GRADE 1

Reader's and Writer's JOURNAL

LEARNING COMPANY

ISBN-13: 978-0-328-85156-0
ISBN-10: 0-328-85156-6
21 2021

Table of Contents

Name _____

DIRECTIONS Say the word for each picture. Write the letter on the line that spells the first sound in the word.

Children apply grade-level phonics and word analysis skills.

DIRECTIONS Choose a word from below and draw it in the box. Then write a sentence using the word.

escaped   survived

_____

- -

_____

Write in Response to Reading

DIRECTIONS Complete the sentence.
When Stellaluna tries to act like a bird, she feels

_____

- -

_____

- -

_____

- -

_____

 Children demonstrate contextual understanding of Benchmark Vocabulary. Children read text closely and use text evidence in their written answers.

Name _____

DIRECTIONS Write all of the uppercase letters of the alphabet on the lines below.

_____
- -
_____

_____
- -
_____

_____
- -
_____

_____
- -
_____

Writing

Think about the story *Stellaluna*. Draw a picture for the beginning, middle, and end parts of the story. Then choose one part and write a sentence about it on the lines below.

_____
- -
_____

_____
- -
_____

_____
- -
_____

Children practice various conventions of standard English. Children write routinely for a range of tasks, purposes, and audiences.

Unit 1 • Module A • Lesson 1 • 3

Name _____

DIRECTIONS Choose a word from below and draw it in the box. Then write a sentence using the word.

grasped   embarrassing   clumsy

Write in Response to Reading

DIRECTIONS Write your answer on the lines.
What does a real fruit bat do?

_____

_____

_____

_____

Children demonstrate contextual understanding of Benchmark Vocabulary. Children read text closely and use text evidence in their written answers.

Name _____

DIRECTIONS Write all the lowercase letters of the alphabet.

_____

- -

_____

- -

_____

- -

_____

- -

_____

Writing

Think about the relationship between Stellaluna and Mother Bat. Draw a picture that shows their relationship. Write a sentence that tells about the relationship on the lines below.

_____

- -

_____

- -

_____

- -

_____

- -

_____

Children practice various conventions of standard English. Children write routinely for a range of tasks, purposes, and audiences.

DIRECTIONS Say the word for each picture.

Write **a** on the line if the word has the same first sound as

Say the word for each picture. Write **a** on the line
to complete the word.

 Children apply grade-level phonics and word
analysis skills.

Name _____

DIRECTIONS Choose a word from below and draw it in the box. Then write a sentence using the word.

limb   land   perched

_____

- -

_____

Tell something about Mama Bird, Pip, Flitter, Flap, or Stellaluna. Write your answer on the lines below.

_____

- -

_____

- -

_____

- -

_____

Children demonstrate contextual understanding of Benchmark Vocabulary. Children read text closely and use text evidence in their written answers.

Name _____

How Polar Bears Hunt

Polar bears live where it is cold. There is ice all around. They have thick fur. They stay warm. They hunt to live. They walk on ice. They look for seals to eat.

Polar bears use clues to hunt. They look for cracks in the ice. Seals swim under water. They come up for air through the cracks. Seals like the sun. They like the heat. Polar bears can find seals in the sun.

Polar bears can slip on the ice. SPLASH! They can fall into the cold water. Polar bears can swim.

Mama bears teach their cubs how to hunt. Cubs learn that hunting is hard work. They must hunt to grow big and strong.

Name _____

Look for Clues

On page 8, circle all the clues that tell about where the polar bears live.

What is it like where polar bears live? Discuss with a partner how the polar bears can live there.

_____

_____

Ask Questions

Write two questions about polar bears.

1. --

_____

2. --

_____

Make Your Case

On page 8, draw a box around *Mama bears* and underline the words that tell what mother polar bears do for their cubs.

On page 8, find other things that polar bears do. Discuss them with a partner.

Children read text closely and use text evidence in their written answers.

Name _____

DIRECTIONS Write your first and last name.

_____

- -

_____

- -

_____

Writing

Think about an interesting event in *Stellaluna*. Write sentences to tell about the event on the lines below. Remember to include details about the characters.

_____

- -

_____

_____

- -

_____

_____

- -

_____

_____

- -

_____

_____

- -

Children practice various conventions of standard English. Children write routinely for a range of tasks, purposes, and audiences.

Name _____

DIRECTIONS Draw the word below in the box. Then write a sentence using the word.

brave

_____

_____

Write in Response to Reading

DIRECTIONS Complete each sentence.

_____

Frog and Toad are _____

_____

They want to be _____

Children demonstrate contextual understanding of Benchmark Vocabulary. Children read text closely and use text evidence in their written answers.

Name _____

What kinds of animals did we read about?

_____

_____

_____

_____

Think about the events in "Dragons and Giants." Pick one event and draw a picture of it. Then write a sentence that tells about the event on the lines below.

_____

_____

_____

_____

_____

_____

_____

_____

Children practice various conventions of standard English. Children write routinely for a range of tasks, purposes, and audiences.

Name _____

DIRECTIONS Choose a word from below and draw it in the box. Then write a sentence using the word.

mountain   snake

_____

- -

_____

Write in Response to Reading

Frog and Toad go up a mountain and see a hawk.

_____

- -

I would like to go   _____

_____

- -

I would like to see   _____

Children demonstrate contextual understanding of Benchmark Vocabulary. Children read text closely and use text evidence in their written answers.

Name _____

What do Frog and Toad see in the cave?

_____

- -

_____

- -

_____

Writing

Draw a picture of something Frog and Toad might do together as friends. Then write a sentence that tells about their friendship on the lines below.

_____

- -

_____

- -

_____

- -

_____

- -

_____

Children practice various conventions of standard English. Children write routinely for a range of tasks, purposes, and audiences.

Name _____

DIRECTIONS Say the word for each picture. Write the letter on the line that spells the first sound in the word.

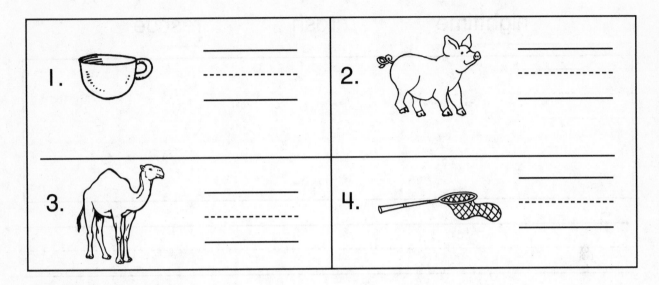

1. _____

2. _____

3. _____

4. _____

Say the word for each picture. Write the letter on the line that completes each word.

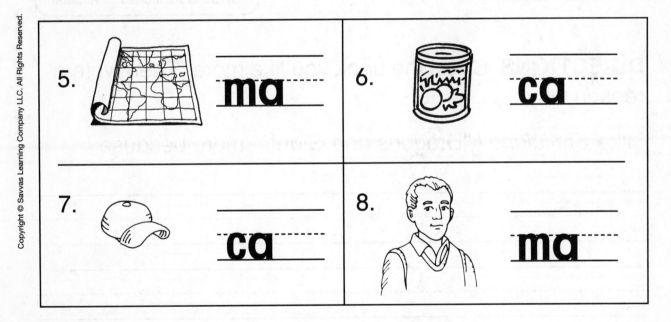

5. **ma** _____

6. **ca** _____

7. **ca** _____

8. **ma** _____

Children apply grade-level phonics and word analysis skills.

Name _____

DIRECTIONS Choose a word from below and draw it in the box. Then write a sentence using the word.

nighttime   crash   rescue

```



```
_____
- -
_____

DIRECTIONS Circle the book you like more. Then write a reason why.

I like *Stellaluna* / "Dragons and Giants" more because

_____
- -
_____
- -
_____

Children demonstrate contextual understanding of Benchmark Vocabulary. Children read text closely and use text evidence in their written answers.

Name _____

DIRECTIONS Circle the words that compare the characters. Then draw a picture to show how the characters are alike.

1. Frog, Toad, and Stellaluna are   animals   people.

2. Frog, Toad, and Stellaluna are   good   bad   friends.

Children analyze and respond to literary texts.

Name _____

What kind of animal is Stellaluna?

_____

- -

_____

- -

_____

- -

_____

Writing

Think about an event from *Stellaluna* or "Dragons and Giants." Write what happens on the lines below. Use details.

_____

- -

_____

- -

_____

- -

_____

- -

_____

- -

_____

Children practice various conventions of standard English. Children write routinely for a range of tasks, purposes, and audiences.

Lesson 7

Name _____

Benchmark Vocabulary

DIRECTIONS Choose a word from below and draw it in the box. Then write a sentence using the word.

clutched   trembling

Write in Response to Reading

DIRECTIONS Complete the sentence to tell what happens in *Stellaluna*.

When the owl attacks, Mother Bat _____

Children demonstrate contextual understanding of Benchmark Vocabulary. Children read text closely and use text evidence in their written answers.

Name _____

DIRECTIONS Write interesting words you know or read in *Stellaluna*. Draw a picture for each word.

  Children analyze and respond to literary texts.

Name _____

DIRECTIONS Circle the complete simple sentence. Write a complete sentence on the line below.

The birds grew up.

Stellaluna

_____

- -

_____

_____

- -

_____

Writing

Draw a picture of one scene from *Stellaluna*. Write details about a character from the scene on the lines below.

_____

- -

_____

_____

- -

_____

_____

- -

_____

Children practice various conventions of standard English. Children write routinely for a range of tasks, purposes, and audiences.

Name _____

DIRECTIONS Say the word for each picture.
Write **a** on the line if the word has the same middle sound as

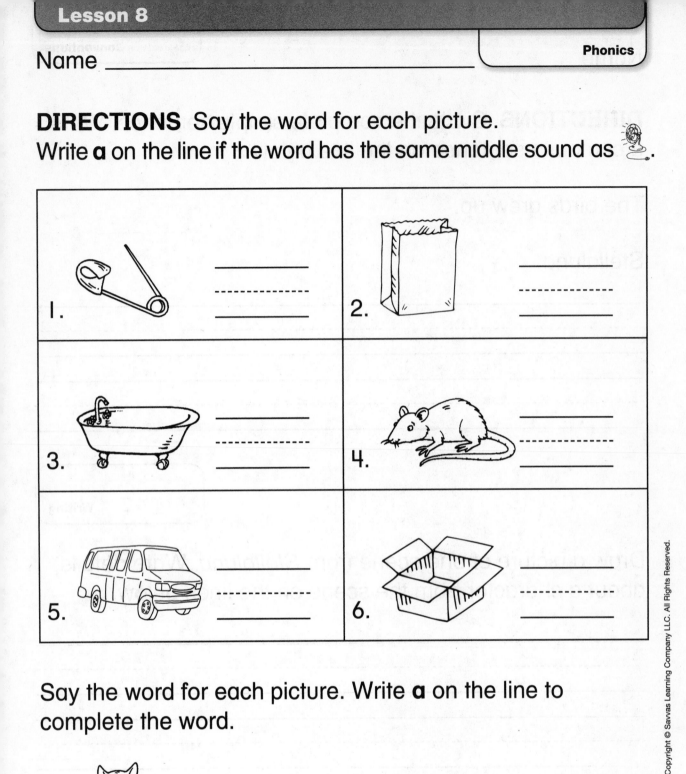

1. _____

2. _____

3. _____

4. _____

5. _____

6. _____

Say the word for each picture. Write **a** on the line to
complete the word.

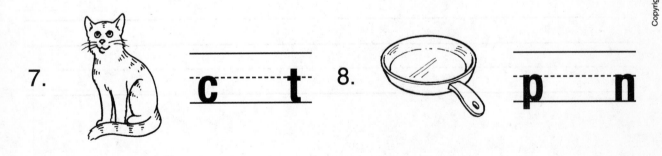

7. c _____ t

8. p _____ n

Children apply grade-level phonics and word
analysis skills.

Name _____

DIRECTIONS Choose a word from below and draw it in the box. Then write a sentence using the word.

daybreak   headfirst

_____

_____

- -

_____

Write in Response to Reading

DIRECTIONS Draw a picture of where Stellaluna lives.

Children demonstrate contextual understanding of Benchmark Vocabulary. Children read text closely and use text evidence in their written answers.

Name _____

DIRECTIONS Add the correct end mark to the sentences.

Bats hang upside down _____

Stellaluna falls into a nest _____

Writing

Choose one setting from *Stellaluna*. Draw a picture of it. Then write about the setting on the lines below.

_____
_____
_____
_____
_____
_____
_____
_____

Children practice various conventions of standard English. Children write routinely for a range of tasks, purposes, and audiences.

Name _____

DIRECTIONS Choose a word from below and draw it in the box. Then write a sentence using the word.

obey   rules   behaved

_____
- -
_____

Write in Response to Reading

DIRECTIONS Complete the sentence.

_____
- -

I think Mother Bat feels _____

when she finds Stellaluna.

Children demonstrate contextual understanding of Benchmark Vocabulary. Children read text closely and use text evidence in their written answers.

Name _____

DIRECTIONS Add the correct end mark to the sentences.

Do you like bats _____

Can Stellaluna hang by her feet _____

Writing

Draw a picture of one event from *Stellaluna*. Write a sentence about it on the lines below. Be sure to include details.

Children practice various conventions of standard English. Children write routinely for a range of tasks, purposes, and audiences.

Name _____

DIRECTIONS Draw the word below in the box. Then write a sentence using the word.

safe

_____

- -

_____

Write in Response to Reading

DIRECTIONS Complete each sentence to tell how Frog and Toad feel at the end of the story.

_____

They are _____

_____

They are _____

Children demonstrate contextual understanding of Benchmark Vocabulary. Children read text closely and use text evidence in their written answers.

Name _____

DIRECTIONS Add the correct end mark to the sentences.

Look out _____

That is a big snake _____

Use the space below to sketch events to plan your writing.

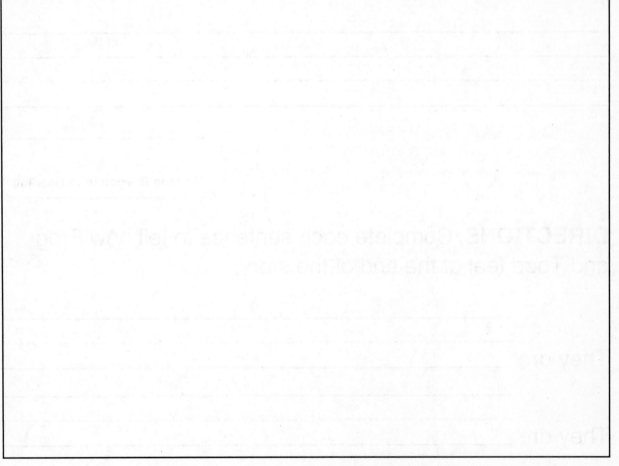

 Children practice various conventions of standard English. Children write routinely for a range of tasks, purposes, and audiences.

Name _____

DIRECTIONS Say the word for each picture. Write the letter on the line that spells the first sound in the word.

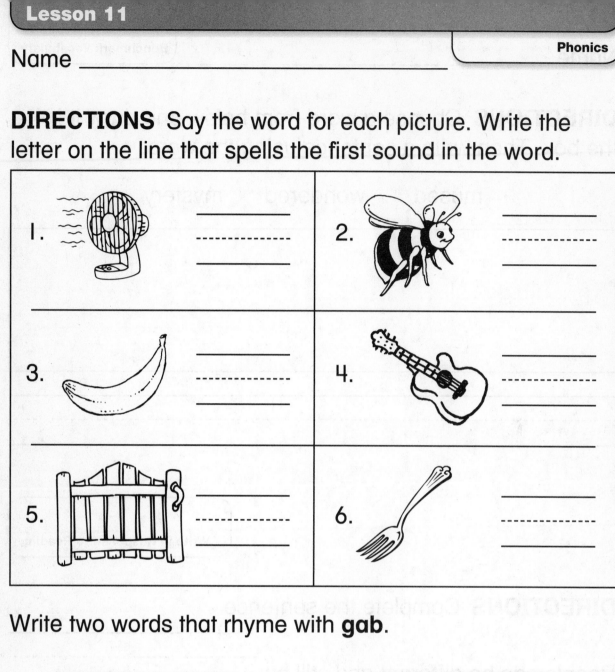

1. _____

2. _____

3. _____

4. _____

5. _____

6. _____

Write two words that rhyme with **gab**.

7. **c** _____

8. **t** _____

Children apply grade-level phonics and word analysis skills.

Name _____

DIRECTIONS Choose a word from below and draw it in the box. Then write a sentence using the word.

mused   wondered   mystery

_____

- -

_____

Write in Response to Reading

DIRECTIONS Complete the sentence.

_____

- -

People can be different and still be _____

_____

- -

_____

- -

_____

Children demonstrate contextual understanding of Benchmark Vocabulary. Children read text closely and use text evidence in their written answers.

Name _____

DIRECTIONS Write or draw a picture to tell the central message of *Stellaluna*.

How Stellaluna and the birds are alike	How Stellaluna and the birds are different

The birds and Stellaluna both feel

Central Message of *Stellaluna*

Children analyze and respond to literary texts.

Name _____

DIRECTIONS Write each sentence correctly.

bats hang upside down.

_____

- -

_____

The birds and stellaluna are friends.

_____

- -

_____

Use your drawings to write about Frog and Toad's friendship. Write a sentence about each drawing.

_____

- -

_____

- -

_____

- -

Children practice various conventions of standard English. Children write routinely for a range of tasks, purposes, and audiences.

Name _____

DIRECTIONS Draw the word below in the box. Then write a sentence using the word.

together

_____

\- -

_____

Write in Response to Reading

DIRECTIONS Tell about the central message of "Dragons and Giants."

Friends are _____

Children demonstrate contextual understanding of Benchmark Vocabulary. Children read text closely and use text evidence in their written answers.

Name _____

DIRECTIONS Circle the complete sentence. Then write your own.

The snake opens its mouth.

opens its mouth

_____

_____

_____

DIRECTIONS Revise and edit your story.

_____

_____

_____

_____

_____

_____

_____

Children practice various conventions of standard English. Children write routinely for a range of tasks, purposes, and audiences.

Name _____

DIRECTIONS Say the word for each picture. Write **i** on the line if the word has the same first sound as 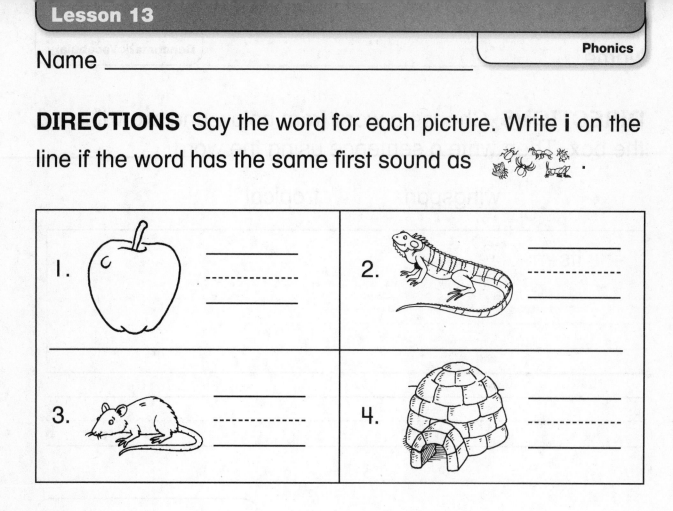 .

Say the word for each picture. Write **i** on the line if the word has the same middle sound as 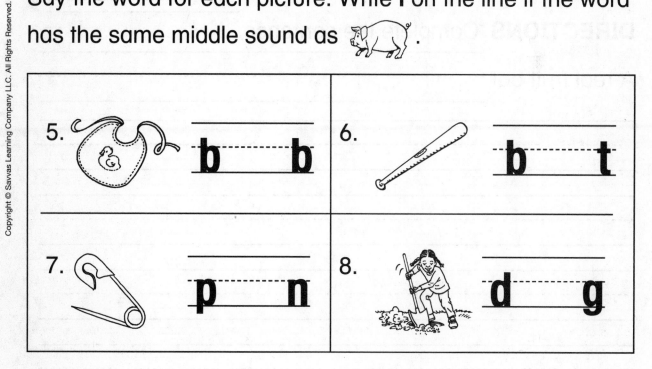 .

Children apply grade-level phonics and word analysis skills.

Name _____

DIRECTIONS Choose a word from below and draw it in the box. Then write a sentence using the word.

wingspan   tropical

Write in Response to Reading

DIRECTIONS Complete the sentence.

A real fruit bat --

Children demonstrate contextual understanding of Benchmark Vocabulary. Children read text closely and use text evidence in their written answers.

Name _____

A New Family

One March day, Ben and Dad went into the garage. Ben saw something odd. It was high up, on the garage door motor.

"A bird's nest!" Ben cried.

It was made of sticks, grass, and feathers. A mother robin flew out. Dad got a ladder. He saw three tiny blue eggs inside the nest.

"What a funny place for a nest!" Ben said.

"It is warm and safe," Dad said. "We'll park the car outside. We'll leave the garage door open so the robin can get food." Dad moved the car.

Ben checked the nest every day. The mother was often there. After two weeks, the eggs hatched. The tiny birds had no feathers. Every day the mother bird brought worms, and the babies got bigger. Soon they had feathers. One day Ben looked in the nest. The baby birds were gone! Ben was glad he had gotten to know the bird family.

Children read text closely and use text evidence in their written answers.

Name _____

Look for Clues

Draw your own pictures of bird eggs in a nest, baby birds, and an adult bird. Add arrows to show the order of events.

Ask Questions

Write a question you have for Ben or Dad about the birds.

_____

_____

Make Your Case

On page 37, draw two circles around something you learned from the story.

_____

_____

Do you think the story is better with or without the pictures? Tell a partner what you think and why you think so.

Children read text closely and use text evidence in their written answers.

Name _____

DIRECTIONS Write a sentence that tells something. Then write a question or exclamation. Use a capital letter. Add an end mark.

_____
- -
_____
_____
- -
_____
_____
- -
_____

Writing

DIRECTIONS Publish your story. Write a title. Draw a picture for the cover.

_____
- -
_____

Children practice various conventions of standard English. Children write routinely for a range of tasks, purposes, and audiences.

Name _____

DIRECTIONS Say the word for each picture. Write the letter on the line that spells the first sound in the word.

1. _____

2. _____

3. _____

4. _____

5. _____

6. _____

7. _____

8. _____

 Children apply grade-level phonics and word analysis skills.

Name _____

DIRECTIONS Choose a word from below and draw it in the box. Then write a sentence using the word.

time   sleep

_____
- -
_____

Write in Response to Reading

DIRECTIONS Write your answer on the line.
What do ducks do with their legs when they sleep?

_____
- -
_____
- -
_____
- -
_____
- -

Children demonstrate contextual understanding of Benchmark Vocabulary. Children read text closely and use text evidence in their written answers.

DIRECTIONS Answer the questions. Then write where you found the answers.

1. What animals like to sleep a lot?

_____

_____ and

_____

_____ like to sleep a lot.

2. I found the answers on pages _____ and _____.

3. How do bats sleep?

_____

_____ hang

_____

by their _____.

4. I found the answers on page _____.

Children analyze and respond to informational texts.

Name _____

DIRECTIONS Circle the nouns. Underline the verbs.

The duck swims around.

Horses run fast.

The cat sleeps quietly.

Writing

Think about two things you learned from *Time to Sleep*. Draw a picture that shows what you learned. Write a sentence that tells about your picture on the lines below.

_____

- -

_____

- -

_____

- -

_____

- -

_____

- -

_____

- -

Children practice various conventions of standard English. Children write routinely for a range of tasks, purposes, and audiences.

DIRECTIONS Draw the word below in the box. Then write a sentence using the word.

animals

Write in Response to Reading

DIRECTIONS Complete each sentence using a word from the box.

Ducks	Bats

_____

- -

_____ sleep on one leg.

_____

- -

_____ sleep upside down.

 Children demonstrate contextual understanding of Benchmark Vocabulary. Children read text closely and use text evidence in their written answers.

Name _____

DIRECTIONS Circle the nouns in the sentences below.

Dolphins sleep with one eye open.

Koalas sleep in trees.

Writing

DIRECTIONS Write a sentence that tells about a photograph from *Time to Sleep*. Then write a heading.

_____

_____

_____

_____

_____

_____

_____

_____

_____

Children practice various conventions of standard English. Children write routinely for a range of tasks, purposes, and audiences.

Name _____

DIRECTIONS Say the word for each picture.
Write **o** on the line if the word has the same first sound as .

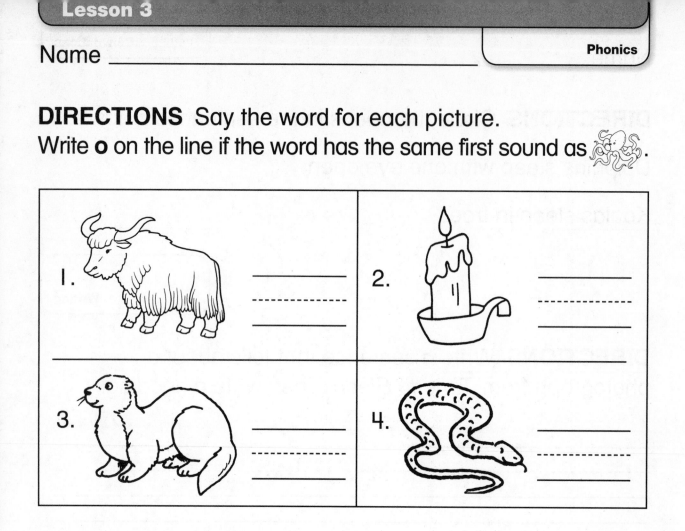

1. _____

2. _____

3. _____

4. _____

Say the word for each picture. Write **o** on the line if the
word has the same middle sound as ●.

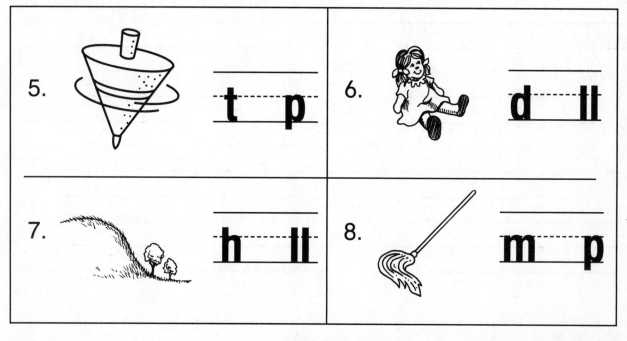

5. _____ **t** ___ **p**

6. _____ **d** ___ **ll**

7. _____ **h** ___ **ll**

8. _____ **m** ___ **p**

Children apply grade-level phonics and word analysis skills.

Name _____

DIRECTIONS Draw a picture of the word below in the box. Then write a sentence using the word.

sorts

Write in Response to Reading

DIRECTIONS Think about the different ways that people and animals sleep. Write a way that people and animals sleep differently.

Some animals sleep _____

Children demonstrate contextual understanding of Benchmark Vocabulary. Children read text closely and use text evidence in their written answers.

Name _____

DIRECTIONS Draw a picture of the main topic of *Time to Sleep*. Then answer the questions below.

```
┌─────────────────────────────────────────┐
│                                         │
│                                         │
│                                         │
│                                         │
│                                         │
└─────────────────────────────────────────┘
```

What is the main topic of *Time to Sleep?*

_____

- -

_____

- -

_____

- -

_____

Retell one detail that supports the main topic.

_____

- -

_____

- -

_____

- -

_____

Children analyze and respond to informational texts.

Name _____

DIRECTIONS Circle the proper nouns. Underline the common nouns.

My dog Jack sleeps on the couch.

Many koalas live in Australia.

Henry enjoys looking at birds.

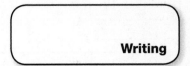

Writing

DIRECTIONS Think of questions you have about the text. Write one of your questions. Then write a sentence to answer the question.

_____

Question: _____

_____

_____

_____

Answer: _____

_____

_____

Children practice various conventions of standard English. Children write routinely for a range of tasks, purposes, and audiences.

Name _____

DIRECTIONS Choose a word or phrase from below and draw it in the box. Then write a sentence using the word or phrase.

upside down   scared

Write in Response to Reading

DIRECTIONS Draw a picture to show how bats sleep. Then write a sentence to describe your picture on the lines below.

Children demonstrate contextual understanding of Benchmark Vocabulary. Children read text closely and use text evidence in their written answers.

Name _____

DIRECTIONS Circle the verbs in the sentences below.

Birds sleep in trees.

Bunnies hop with their feet.

Bees fly away.

DIRECTIONS Draw two things you learned about how animals sleep. Then write a sentence about one of your drawings on the lines below.

_____
- -
_____
- -
_____
- -
_____
- -
_____
- -
_____
- -
_____

Children practice various conventions of standard English. Children write routinely for a range of tasks, purposes, and audiences.

Name _____

DIRECTIONS Draw a picture of the word below in the box. Then write a sentence using the word.

lock

```



```

_____

- -

_____

Write in Response to Reading

DIRECTIONS Use the word bank to complete the sentences.

| lock their legs | standing up |

_____
- -

Horses can sleep _____.

_____
- -

Horses _____

so they do not fall over.

Children demonstrate contextual understanding of Benchmark Vocabulary. Children read text closely and use text evidence in their written answers.

Name _____

DIRECTIONS Change the singular nouns to plural nouns by adding an **s**. Rewrite the words on the lines.

_____

cat_____

_____

duck_____

_____

_____

_____

_____

Writing

Think about the main topic and key details on pages 6–7 in *Time to Sleep*. Complete the graphic organizer.

Main Idea

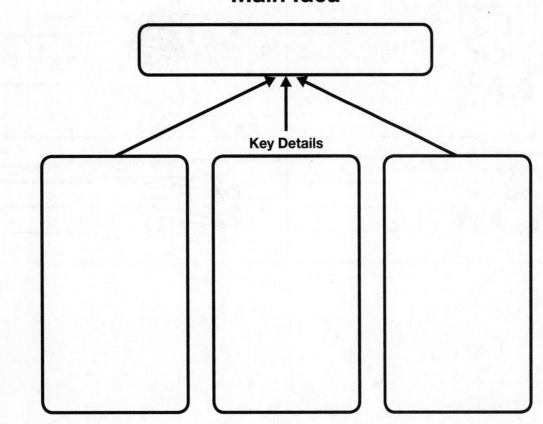

Key Details

Children practice various conventions of standard English. Children write routinely for a range of tasks, purposes, and audiences.

Name _____

DIRECTIONS Say the word for each picture. Write the letter on the line that spells the first sound in the word.

1.

2.

3.

4.

5.

6.

7.

8.

 Children apply grade-level phonics and word analysis skills.

Name _____

DIRECTIONS Choose a word from below and draw it in the box. Then write a sentence using the word.

danger   tuck

_____

- -

_____

Write in Response to Reading

Why do dolphins sleep with one eye open?

_____

- -

_____

- -

_____

- -

_____

- -

_____

Children demonstrate contextual understanding of Benchmark Vocabulary. Children read text closely and use text evidence in their written answers.

DIRECTIONS Circle the verbs that match the nouns.

| Dolphins | look/looks | out for danger. |
| A dolphin | look/looks | out for danger. |

Writing

Read your question and think about the answer. Write a sentence that answers the question on the lines below.

_____

- -

_____

- -

_____

- -

_____

- -

_____

- -

_____

- -

_____

 Children practice various conventions of standard English. Children write routinely for a range of tasks, purposes, and audiences.

Name _____

DIRECTIONS Choose a word from below and draw it in the box. Then write a sentence using the word.

day   high   anywhere

_____

_____

Write in Response to Reading

Why do koalas sleep in trees?

_____

_____

_____

_____

Children demonstrate contextual understanding of Benchmark Vocabulary. Children read text closely and use text evidence in their written answers.

Name _____

DIRECTIONS Circle the verbs that match the nouns.

A koala   live / lives   in the tree.

Koalas   live / lives   in the tree.

Writing

Think about the question your group chose. Then think about the answer your group drew. Write a sentence that tells the answer to the question on the lines below.

_____

- -

_____

- -

_____

- -

_____

- -

_____

- -

_____

- -

_____

Children practice various conventions of standard English. Children write routinely for a range of tasks, purposes, and audiences.

Lesson 8

Phonics

Name _____

DIRECTIONS Say the word for each picture. Write **e** on the line if the word has the same first sound as  .

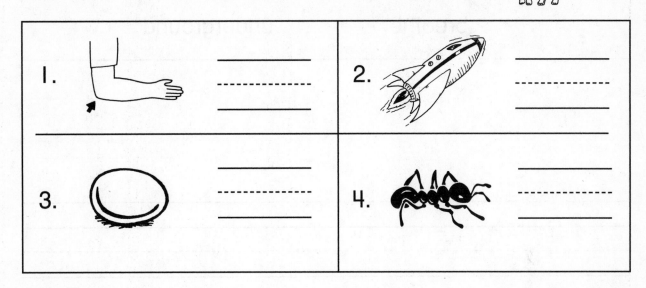

1. _____

2. _____

3. _____

4. _____

Say the word for each picture. Write **e** on the line if the word has the same middle sound as .

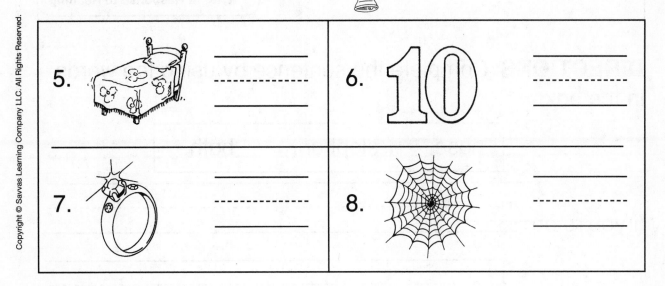

5. _____

6. _____

7. _____

8. _____

Children apply grade-level phonics and word analysis skills.

Name _____

DIRECTIONS Choose a word from below and draw it in the box. Then write a sentence using the word.

breathe   underground

_____

- -

_____

Write in Response to Reading

DIRECTIONS Complete the sentence by using the words in the box.

nose	elephant	bath

If you're an _____,

you use your _____

to give yourself a _____.

Children demonstrate contextual understanding of Benchmark Vocabulary. Children read text closely and use text evidence in their written answers.

Name _____

A Happy Ending

Once there was a baby bird. He grew up with a family of ducks. He didn't look like them, though. He was fuzzy and gray. The other ducks called him ugly. One day the ducks got a big surprise. The baby bird had grown up. He had turned beautiful. His feathers were as white as snow. He was really a swan!

That is the tale of the ugly duckling. Ducks are different from swans. Grown-up swans often have bright white feathers. They have long, curved necks. Baby swans look different.

A mother swan lays from three to nine eggs. After five weeks, the eggs hatch. A baby swan has gray feathers and a short neck.

Just as in the story, the baby swan has a happy ending. As the baby grows, it changes. After a year, its feathers become white. Its neck gets long. The "ugly" baby becomes a graceful swan!

Children read text closely to determine what the text says.

Look for Clues

Draw a picture of a duck and a swan. Draw arrows to show two ways ducks and swans are different.

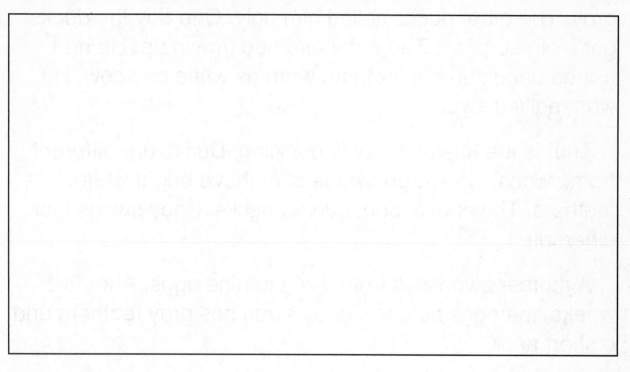

Ask Questions

On page 61, underline a sentence in the text that you would like to know more about.

Make Your Case

At the beginning of page 61, draw a box around something you learned from the story about the ugly duckling.

 Children read text closely to determine what the text says.

Name _____

DIRECTIONS Complete the sentences below by adding a question word at the beginning and a question mark at the end.

Who	What	When	Where	Why	How

_____   _____

_____ do you get to school _____

_____   _____

_____ is your favorite color _____

Writing

DIRECTIONS Draw one animal from the text. Write a question about the animal. Then write an answer to that question. _____

Question: _____

_____

_____

Answer: _____

_____

_____

Children practice various conventions of standard English. Children write routinely for a range of tasks, purposes, and audiences.

Name _____

DIRECTIONS Choose a word from below and draw it in the box. Then write a sentence using the word.

hang   high   feet   eyes

Write in Response to Reading

DIRECTIONS Write your answers on the lines.

What can animals do with their feet?

1. A duck can _____

2. A water strider can _____

Children demonstrate contextual understanding of Benchmark Vocabulary. Children read text closely and use text evidence in their written answers.

Name _____

DIRECTIONS Write the question below correctly.

what do you do with your nose

_____

_____

_____

_____

Writing

DIRECTIONS How do animals use their body parts? Think about what you learned from the texts. Write 2 facts on the lines below.

Fact 1

_____

_____

_____

Fact 2

_____

_____

_____

Children practice various conventions of standard English. Children write routinely for a range of tasks, purposes, and audiences.

Name _____

DIRECTIONS Choose a word from below and draw it in the box. Then write a sentence using the word.

pesky   warn

_____

- -

Write in Response to Reading

DIRECTIONS Write a sentence about how an animal uses its tail.

_____

- -

_____

- -

_____

- -

_____

- -

_____

Children demonstrate contextual understanding of Benchmark Vocabulary. Children read text closely and use text evidence in their written answers.

Name _____

DIRECTIONS Circle the common nouns. Underline the proper nouns.

turtle   Swan Lake   pencil   Mr. Smith

New York   May   cats   pool

Draw a picture of an animal you will ask a question about. Plan your writing. Write a question about your animal.

_____
- -
_____
- -
_____
- -
_____
- -
_____
- -
_____

Children practice various conventions of standard English. Children write routinely for a range of tasks, purposes, and audiences.

Name _____

DIRECTIONS Say the word for each picture. Write the letter or letters on the line that spells the first sound in the word.

1. _____

2. _____

3. _____

4. _____

5. _____

6. _____

7. _____

8. _____

Children apply grade-level phonics and word analysis skills.

Name _____

DIRECTIONS Choose a word from below and draw it in the box. Then write a sentence using the word.

spot   squirt

```



```

_____

- -

_____

Write in Response to Reading

DIRECTIONS Draw a picture of the answer. Then write the answer on the line below.

What can a lizard do with its tail?

```



```

_____

- -

_____

_____

- -

_____

Children demonstrate contextual understanding of Benchmark Vocabulary. Children read text closely and use text evidence in their written answers.

Name _____

DIRECTIONS Read the words in the box. Choose the best word to answer the question or complete the sentence.

| bat | giraffe | humpback whale | tail | tree |

1. Which animal brushes flies off with its tail?

_____

_____

_____

----

2. What happens after a skunk lifts its _____ ?
   It sprays a stinky spray.

_____

----

3. How does a _____ use its ears?
   It uses its ears to see.

4. What uses its ears to hear sounds hundreds
   of miles away?

_____

_____

5. Where does a monkey use its tail?   _____

   The monkey uses its tail to hang from a _____.

Children analyze and respond to informational texts.

Name _____

DIRECTIONS Complete the sentence by adding **-s** or **-es** to the action verb.

hunt An eagle _____ small animals.

catch A pelican _____ fish with its mouth.

Writing

Write your question about an animal.

_____
_____
_____

Write the answer to your question.

_____
_____
_____

Children practice various conventions of standard English. Children write routinely for a range of tasks, purposes, and audiences.

Name _____

DIRECTIONS Choose a word from below and draw it in the box. Then write a sentence using the word.

sticky   scoop   swallow

[box]

_____

- -

Write in Response to Reading

Draw the animal with the most interesting mouth.

[box]

Why is this mouth interesting?

_____

- -

_____

- -

 Children demonstrate contextual understanding of Benchmark Vocabulary. Children read text closely and use text evidence in their written answers.

Name _____

DIRECTIONS Draw a picture of a pelican. Show how the pelican eats a fish.

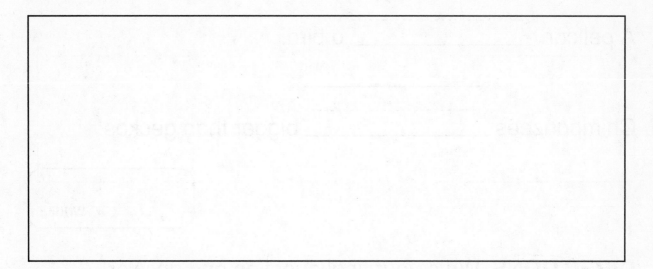

Write words or sentences to explain your drawing.

_____
- -
_____
- -
_____
- -
_____
- -
_____
- -
_____

Children analyze and respond to informational texts.

Name _____

DIRECTIONS Complete the sentences with **is** or **are**.

_____

A pelican _____ a bird.

_____

Chimpanzees _____ bigger than geckos.

Writing

DIRECTIONS Write your final question and answer.
Use your best handwriting.

_____

_____

_____

_____

_____

_____

_____

_____

Children practice various conventions of standard
English. Children write routinely for a range of tasks,
purposes, and audiences.

Name _____

DIRECTIONS Say the word for each picture. Write **u** on the line if the word has the same first sound as .

1. ___ ___ ___
2. ___ ___ ___
3. ___ ___ ___
4. ___ ___ ___

Say the word for each picture. Write **u** on the line if the word has the same middle sound as ⬭ .

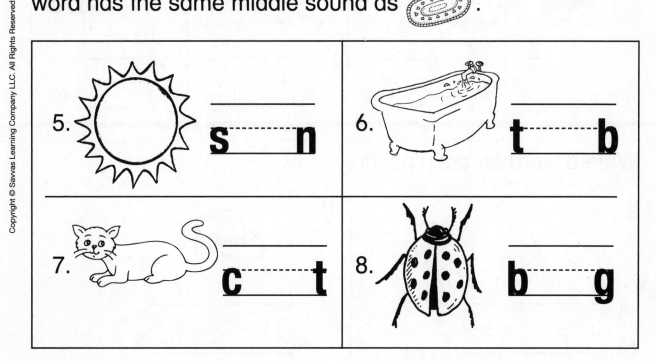

5. **s** ___ **n**
6. **t** ___ **b**
7. **c** ___ **t**
8. **b** ___ **g**

Children apply grade-level phonics and word analysis skills.

Name _____

DIRECTIONS Say the word for each picture.
Write **a** on the line if you hear the **short a** sound.

c_a_t

1. _____
   ----
   b ____ g

2. _____
   ----
   f ____ n

3. _____
   ----
   m ____ p

4. _____
   ----
   m ____ p

5. _____
   ----
   c ____ n

6. _____
   ----
   m ____ n

7. _____
   ----
   p ____ g

8. _____
   ----
   v ____ n

Write a word for each picture.

9. _____
   ----

10. _____

 Children apply grade-level phonics and word analysis skills.

Name _____

DIRECTIONS Choose a word from below and draw it in the box. Then write a sentence using the word.

learning   proud

```
┌──────────────────────────────────────────────────┐
│                                                    │
│                                                    │
│                                                    │
│                                                    │
│                                                    │
│                                                    │
└──────────────────────────────────────────────────┘
```

_____

_____

Write in Response to Reading

DIRECTIONS Draw a picture that shows one character, setting, and major event from *A Fine, Fine School.* Then write the character, setting, and event on the lines below.

_____

Character: _____

_____

Setting: _____

_____

Event: _____

Children demonstrate contextual understanding of Benchmark Vocabulary. Children read closely and use text evidence in their written answers.

Name _____

DIRECTIONS Rewrite the sentence below correctly.

my three favorite colors are red yellow and blue

_____

_____

_____

Writing

DIRECTIONS Name the topic. Write one fact and one opinion about Mr. Keene.

Topic: _____

Fact: Mr. Keene _____

_____

Opinion: I think Mr. Keene _____

_____

Children practice various conventions of standard English. Children write routinely for a range of tasks, purposes, and audiences.

Name _____

DIRECTIONS Choose a word from below and draw it in the box. Then write a sentence using the word.

strolled   waved

_____

- -

_____

Write in Response to Reading

DIRECTIONS Write three things Tillie does with her brother.

_____

- -

_____

- -

_____

- -

_____

- -

_____

Children demonstrate contextual understanding of Benchmark Vocabulary. Children read text closely and use text evidence in their written answers.

Name _____

DIRECTIONS Circle the word that tells what is happening now. Underline the words that tell what will happen. Put an X on the word that tells what already happened.

Tillie eats lunch at school.

Mr. Keene walked in the halls.

Beans will wait for Tillie at home.

Writing

DIRECTIONS Look back at your opinion of Mr. Keene on page 78. Why do you think or feel that way? Write your reason using an example from the story.

I think Mr. Keene _____

_____

_____

because _____

_____

_____

_____

_____

Children practice various conventions of standard English. Children write routinely for a range of tasks, purposes, and audiences.

Name _____

DIRECTIONS Say the word for each picture. Write **ck** on the line if the word has the same ending sound as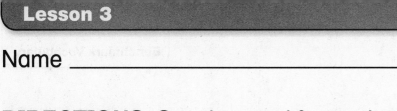

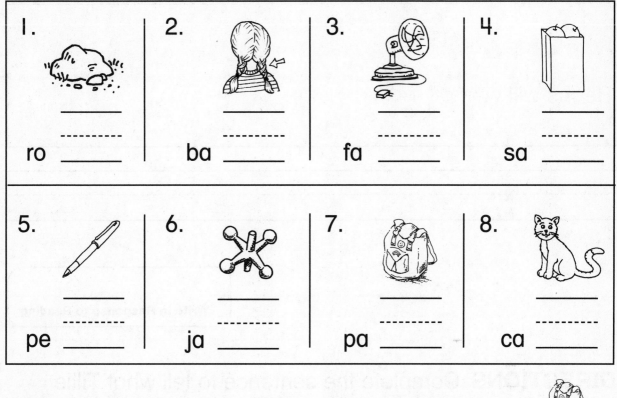

1. ro _____

2. ba _____

3. fa _____

4. sa _____

5. pe _____

6. ja _____

7. pa _____

8. ca _____

Write two words that have the same ending sound as .

_____   _____

_____   _____

Children apply grade-level phonics and word analysis skills.

Name _____

DIRECTIONS Choose a word from below and draw it in the box. Then write a sentence using the word.

announced   everything

```




```
_____

- -

_____

Write in Response to Reading

DIRECTIONS Complete the sentence to tell what Tillie does at school.

_____

- -

Tillie _____

_____

- -

_____

_____

- -

_____ at school.

Children demonstrate contextual understanding of Benchmark Vocabulary. Children read text closely and use text evidence in their written answers.

Name _____

At the Rodeo

Have you ever seen a bucking bronco? How about a cowboy roping a calf? Come to the rodeo!

Rodeo cowboys and cowgirls show their skills. Cowboys on a ranch have these skills. First is the Grand Entry. The cowboys and cowgirls gallop into the arena on their horses. They carry American flags. It is exciting!

Next, the cowboys rope calves. A cowboy on a horse twirls his lariat. A lariat is a long rope with a loop on the end. He must quickly catch a calf with the rope. Real cowboys do this job on a ranch.

Then rodeo clowns come out. They wear Western clothes and clown makeup. They're funny! Next is bronc riding. The bronc is chosen because it acts like a wild horse. The cowboy holds on to the horse with one strap. He tries to stay on. The cowboy who stays on longest wins.

Rodeos started long ago. Cowboys were the biggest stars in the West. Rodeos are still fun!

Children read text closely to determine what the text says.

Name _____

Look for Clues

On page 83, circle the action words that show what cowboys and cowgirls are able to do.

Ask Questions

On page 83, find the rodeo event that you have questions about. Underline it.

Make Your Case

Circle the word in this sentence that tells how the writer feels about the rodeo: The rodeo is scary/fun.

Make Your Case: Extend Your Ideas

Write how you feel about the rodeo. Finish the sentence:

_____

- -

The rodeo is _____ .

Does your answer show you agree with the writer? Why or why not?

 Children read text closely to determine what the text says.

Name _____

DIRECTIONS Circle the words that need capital letters. Then write the sentence.

jane will have a party on july 4.

_____

- -

_____

- -

_____

Writing

DIRECTIONS Write an opinion about a character in *A Fine, Fine School.*

I think _____

_____

is _____ because

_____

- -

_____

- -

_____.

 Children practice various conventions of standard English. Children write routinely for a range of tasks, purposes, and audiences.

Name _____

DIRECTIONS Choose a word from below and draw it in the box. Then write a sentence using the word.

office   worried

_____

- -

_____

Write in Response to Reading

DIRECTIONS Choose one character from *A Fine, Fine School.* Write about the character on the lines below.

_____

- -

_____

- -

_____

- -

_____

 Children demonstrate contextual understanding of Benchmark Vocabulary. Children read text closely and use text evidence in their written answers.

Name _____

DIRECTIONS Add " " to each sentence.

Come here, Tillie said.

We don't want school in the summer,   the teachers said.

DIRECTIONS Pretend you are a character from *A Fine, Fine School*. You talk to Mr. Keene about his decision to have more school. Complete the sentence below.

_____

Mr. Keene, I think _____

_____

_____

_____

_____

_____

_____

_____

_____

_____

Children practice various conventions of standard English. Children write routinely for a range of tasks, purposes, and audiences.

Name _____

DIRECTIONS Choose a word from below and draw it in the box. Then write a sentence using the word.

enormous   cheer

Write in Response to Reading

DIRECTIONS Complete the sentence.

Mr. Keene says there will be no school on the weekends, holidays, or summer. I think this makes Tillie feel

_____

_____ because

Children demonstrate contextual understanding of Benchmark Vocabulary. Children read text closely and use text evidence in their written answers.

Name _____

DIRECTIONS Circle the words that describe the nouns. Then write your own sentence with adjectives.

We go to a fine school on a busy street.

_____

_____

_____

_____

Writing

DIRECTIONS Write a reason to support your opinion.

_____

_____

_____

_____

_____

_____

Children practice various conventions of standard English. Children write routinely for a range of tasks, purposes, and audiences.

Name _____

DIRECTIONS Say the word for each picture.
Write **i** on the line if you hear the **short i** sound.

p<u>i</u>g

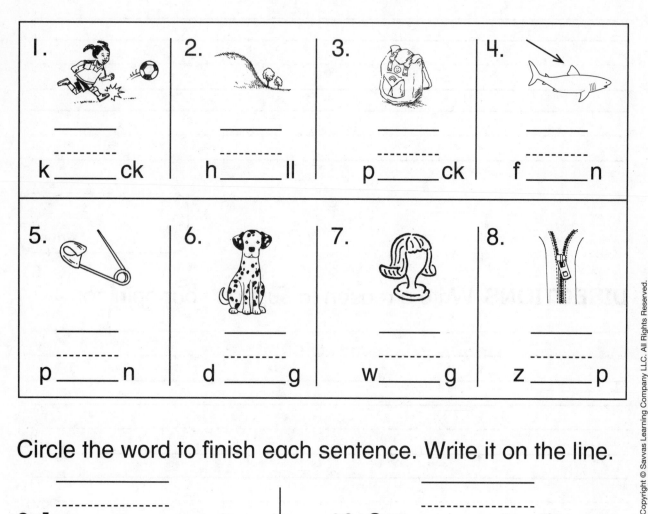

1. _____
k _____ ck

2. _____
h _____ ll

3. _____
p _____ ck

4. _____
f _____ n

5. _____
p _____ n

6. _____
d _____ g

7. _____
w _____ g

8. _____
z _____ p

Circle the word to finish each sentence. Write it on the line.

9. I _____ go.

will   wall

10. Sam _____ the mat.

hip   hid

 Children apply grade-level phonics and word analysis skills.

Name _____

DIRECTIONS Draw the word below in the box. Then write a sentence using the word.

younger

DIRECTIONS Complete the sentence.

The school was fine again because Mr. Keene learned

Children demonstrate contextual understanding of Benchmark Vocabulary. Children read text closely and use text evidence in their written answers.

Name _____

DIRECTIONS Add commas to each sentence.

We use crayons pens and paper at school.

Jane wants to learn about bugs dogs and flowers.

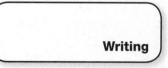

Writing

DIRECTIONS Write your group's opinion about *A Fine, Fine School.*

_____

- -

_____

- -

_____

- -

_____

- -

_____

- -

_____

- -

_____

- -

_____

Children practice various conventions of standard English. Children write routinely for a range of tasks, purposes, and audiences.

Name _____

DIRECTIONS Draw the word below in the box. Then write a sentence using the word.

bullied

_____

_____

DIRECTIONS Complete the sentence.

_____

Mean Jean is _____
_____

_____

_____

Children demonstrate contextual understanding of Benchmark Vocabulary. Children read text closely and use text evidence in their written answers.

Name _____

DIRECTIONS Circle the words or phrases from *The Recess Queen* that appeal to your sense of hearing.

But when the recess bell went ringity-ring,

this kid ran zingity-zing

for the playground gate.

The kid you might scare with a jump

and a "BOO" was too new

to know about Mean Jean the Recess Queen.

Find other words in the story that appeal to your senses. Write them on the lines below.

_____
- -
_____
- -
_____
- -
_____

 Children analyze and respond to literary and informational text.

Name _____

DIRECTIONS Circle the word that shows the action. Then circle when the action happens.

Sue jumped rope with me.   past   present   future

Sue will play with me later.   past   present   future

Writing

DIRECTIONS Write an opinion about one of the characters in *The Recess Queen.*

_____

I think _____

_____

is _____

_____

_____

_____

_____

 Children practice various conventions of standard English. Children write routinely for a range of tasks, purposes, and audiences.

DIRECTIONS Say the word for each picture. Write **x** on the line if the word has the same ending sound as **ax**.

a<u>x</u>

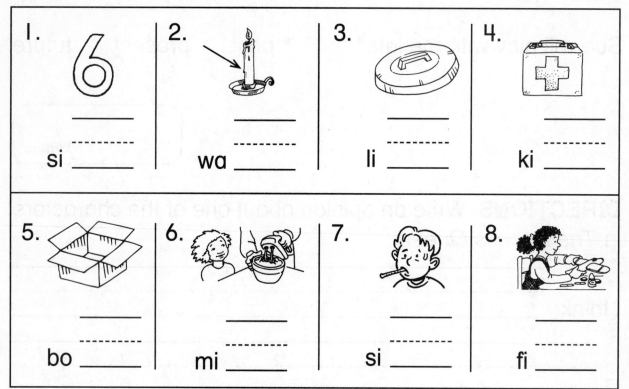

1. si ____

2. wa ____

3. li ____

4. ki ____

5. bo ____

6. mi ____

7. si ____

8. fi ____

Write two words that have the same ending sound as .

_____   _____

_____   _____

Read the sentence below. Underline the words that have the same ending sound as **ax**.

He saw six wax cats.

Children apply grade-level phonics and word analysis skills.

Benchmark Vocabulary

Name _____

DIRECTIONS Draw the word below in the box. Then write a sentence using the word.

nobody

_____

- -

_____

Write in Response to Reading

DIRECTIONS On the school playground, the children jumped. Write a sentence that uses the word *jumped.*

_____

- -

_____

- -

_____

- -

_____

Children demonstrate contextual understanding of Benchmark Vocabulary. Children read text closely and use text evidence in their written answers.

DIRECTIONS Circle the word that can replace the underlined words in the sentence.

I will not tell <u>Sue or Jean.</u>   anywhere   anyone

Jean can go <u>on the swings or the slide.</u>   anywhere   anyone

Writing

DIRECTIONS Rewrite the opinion statement from Lesson 7 on page 95 to include a reason for your opinion.

_____

- -

_____

- -

_____

- -

_____

- -

_____

- -

_____

- -

_____

Children practice various conventions of standard English. Children write routinely for a range of tasks, purposes, and audiences.

Name _____

DIRECTIONS Draw the word below in the box. Then write a sentence using the word.

tiny

```
┌─────────────────────────────────────┐
│                                     │
│                                     │
│                                     │
│                                     │
│                                     │
└─────────────────────────────────────┘
```

_____

- -

_____

Write in Response to Reading

DIRECTIONS Complete the sentence.

_____

- -

Mean Jean has a _____

_____

- -

voice, a _____ voice,

_____

- -

an _____ voice.

Children demonstrate contextual understanding of Benchmark Vocabulary. Children read text closely and use text evidence in their written answers.

Name _____

DIRECTIONS Circle the word that means the book belongs to Sue. Then write a sentence that uses that word.

Sue lost her book.

_____
- -
_____
_____
- -
_____

Writing

DIRECTIONS Write a new opinion about a character or an event. Circle the adjectives you use.

_____
- -
_____
_____
- -
_____
_____
_____
- -
_____
_____
- -
_____

Children practice various conventions of standard English. Children write routinely for a range of tasks, purposes, and audiences.

Name _____

DIRECTIONS Choose a word from below and draw it in the box. Then write a sentence using the word.

snarled   bossy

```
┌─────────────────────────────────────────┐
│                                         │
│                                         │
│                                         │
│                                         │
│                                         │
└─────────────────────────────────────────┘
```

_____

- -

_____

DIRECTIONS Draw a picture of Jean or Katie Sue. Write words that tell about the character.

_____

I drew _____

_____

She is _____

_____

_____

_____

Children demonstrate contextual understanding of Benchmark Vocabulary. Children read text closely and use text evidence in their written answers.

Name _____

DIRECTIONS Circle the name of the person who says or does each thing.

Story Elements: Characters

1. Who growls, howls, snarls, and grabs?

   Jean   Katie Sue

2. Who is puny and loony?

   Jean   Katie Sue

3. Who says "How DID you get so bossy?"

   Jean   Katie Sue

4. Who says "Nobody kicks until Queen Jean kicks?"

   Jean   Katie Sue

Children analyze and respond to literary and informational text.

Name _____

DIRECTIONS Circle the word that describes the noun.

Mean Jean was a bossy girl.

She bullied tiny kids.

Writing

DIRECTIONS Write an opinion statement about your poster.

_____
- -
I think my poster is _____

_____   _____
- - - - - - - - - - -   - - - - - - - - - -
_____ because _____

_____
- -
_____

_____
- -
_____

_____
- -
_____

_____
- -
_____

Children practice various conventions of standard English. Children write routinely for a range of tasks, purposes, and audiences.

Name _____

DIRECTIONS Say the word for each picture.
Write **o** on the line if you hear the **short o** sound.

 t<u>o</u>p

1. p ____ t

2. f ____ x

3. l ____ ck

4. b ____ t

5. w ____ b

6. r ____ ck

7. ____ x

8. d ____ ck

Write a word for each picture.

9.

10.

Children apply grade-level phonics and word analysis skills.

Name _____

DIRECTIONS Choose a word from below and draw it in the box. Then write a sentence using the word.

dared   stared

```



```

_____

DIRECTIONS Complete the sentence with a word that rhymes.

I like ice cream, I like tea, I want you to fly like a

_____

_____

Children demonstrate contextual understanding of Benchmark Vocabulary. Children read text closely and use text evidence in their written answers.

Name _____

DIRECTIONS Read these sentences from *The Recess Queen.* Circle two words that rhyme.

Then from the side a kid called out,

"Go, Jean, go!"

And too surprised to even shout,

Jean jumped in with Katie Sue.

Read the sentences again. Which two lines have the same rhythm? Underline them.

Find two other words that rhyme in the story.
Write them below.

_____

- -

_____

- -

_____

- -

_____

 Children analyze and respond to literary and informational text.

Name _____

DIRECTIONS Complete the sentences using the word
I or *me*.

The kids in my class like _____.

_____ want to play with my friends.

Will you play with _____?

Writing

DIRECTIONS Write the topic of your opinion piece.

_____

_____

_____

_____

_____

_____

_____

_____

_____

_____

_____

Children practice various conventions of
standard English. Children write routinely for a
range of tasks, purposes, and audiences.

Name _____

DIRECTIONS Choose a word from below and draw it in the box. Then write a sentence using the word.

giggled   disaster

```
┌─────────────────────────────────────────┐
│                                         │
│                                         │
│                                         │
│                                         │
└─────────────────────────────────────────┘
```

_____

- -

_____

Write in Response to Reading

DIRECTIONS Complete the sentence to tell what Jean learns.

_____
- -
A friend should _____
_____
- -
_____
_____
- -
A friend should not _____
_____
- -
_____

Children demonstrate contextual understanding of Benchmark Vocabulary. Children read text closely and use text evidence in their written answers.

Name _____

DIRECTIONS Use a word in the box to complete the sentences below.

everyone **everything**

_____

I like _____ about school.

_____

Jean is mean to _____ at school.

DIRECTIONS Write your opinion about one of the texts. Write a reason that supports your opinion.

_____

_____

_____

_____

_____

_____

_____

_____

Children practice various conventions of standard English. Children write routinely for a range of tasks, purposes, and audiences.

Name _____

DIRECTIONS Circle a word to match each picture.

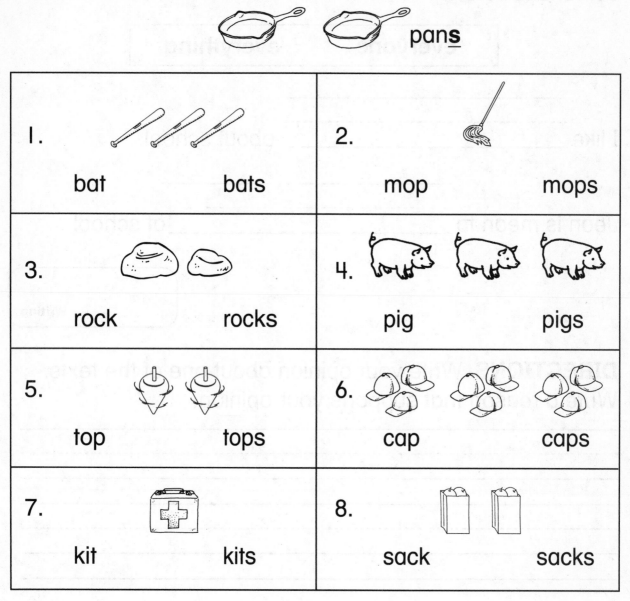

pan**s**

1. bat bats	2. mop mops
3. rock rocks	4. pig pigs
5. top tops	6. cap caps
7. kit kits	8. sack sacks

Write a sentence for each word.

9. cats _____

10. fans _____

 Children apply grade-level phonics and word analysis skills.

Name _____

DIRECTIONS Choose a word from below and draw it in the box. Then write a sentence using the word.

learning   everything

Write in Response to Reading

The endings of *A Fine, Fine School* and *The Recess Queen* are alike in some ways. At the ending of both stories, the characters feel

 Children demonstrate contextual understanding of Benchmark Vocabulary. Children read text closely and use text evidence in their written answers.

Name _____

Children's Day

Today is May 5. It is Children's Day! This is the best holiday.

I put on a kimono. It is like a robe. My sisters and I are lucky. My father works at a kimono factory. We have a lot of kimonos!

The smell of iris flowers fills the air. Today my brother uses the leaves of this plant as a sword. He is dressed like a Japanese warrior called a samurai.

I am excited to help hang paper carp outside. A carp is a kind of fish. Carp are strong. Our parents want us to be strong like carp.

I cannot wait to see my cousins. We go to their house and play games. Then we eat mochi (MOH-chee) rice. It is sweet.

My parents make Children's Day special. They want us to be strong. They have hopes for us. Children's Day is fun and makes me feel proud.

 Children read text closely to determine what the text says.

Name _____

Look for Clues

Circle the sentence that tells what the parents do for Children's Day.

What do the parents want their children to be like?

_____

_____

Ask Questions

On page 112, find the part that you would like to know more about. Draw a box around it.

Make Your Case

On page 112, underline sentences that tell why the girl likes Children's Day.

Would you like to have Children's Day here? Tell a partner what you think and why.

 Children read text closely to determine what the text says.

Name _____

DIRECTIONS Use **but**, **or**, or **so** to complete the sentences below.

Mean Jean was a bully, _____ now she is nice.

She is nice, _____ kids like her.

Writing

DIRECTIONS Write your opinion with at least one detail added to it.

_____

_____

_____

_____

_____

_____

_____

_____

_____

 Children practice various conventions of standard English. Children write routinely for a range of tasks, purposes, and audiences.

Name _____

DIRECTIONS Add **-s** to each word.
Write the new word on the line.

1. hop _____

2. pat _____

3. hug _____

4. dig _____

Use the words you wrote to finish the sentences.
Write the words on the lines.

5. The dog _____ it up.

6. The dog _____ on Jill.

7. Sam _____ the dog.

8. Pam _____ the dog.

Children apply grade-level phonics and word
analysis skills.

Name _____

DIRECTIONS Choose a word from below and draw it in the box. Then write a sentence using the word.

perfect   tidy

Write in Response to Reading

DIRECTIONS Write your answer on the lines below.

Why does Bryan's family move to China?

_____

- - - - - - - - - - - - - - - - - - - -

_____

- - - - - - - - - - - - - - - - - - - -

_____

- - - - - - - - - - - - - - - - - - - -

Children demonstrate contextual understanding of Benchmark Vocabulary. Children read text closely and use text evidence in their written answers.

Name _____

DIRECTIONS Think about what happens at the beginning, in the middle, and at the end of *Far from Home.* Then answer the questions below.

What is one thing that happens at the beginning of the story?

_____

_____

_____

_____

_____

What is one thing that happens in the middle of the story?

_____

_____

_____

_____

_____

What is one thing that happens at the end of the story?

_____

_____

_____

_____

_____

Children analyze and respond to literary texts.

Name _____

DIRECTIONS Circle the action words that tell what Bryan does.

Bryan moves to China.

Bryan uses chopsticks.

Bryan learns kung fu.

Writing

DIRECTIONS Look at the illustration you drew. Write a sentence that tells a fact about your illustration.

_____

_____

_____

_____

_____

_____

_____

_____

_____

 Children practice various conventions of standard English. Children write routinely for a range of tasks, purposes, and audiences.

Name _____

DIRECTIONS Choose a word from below and draw it in the box. Then write a sentence using the word.

tucked   strange

Write in Response to Reading

DIRECTIONS Complete the sentence.

One thing Bryan learns at school is _____

Children demonstrate contextual understanding of Benchmark Vocabulary. Children read text closely and use text evidence in their written answers.

DIRECTIONS Think about what the illustrations on pages 10 and 11 show. Then answer the questions below.

What is one thing you learn about a character from the illustrations?

_____

_____

_____

_____

What is one thing you learn about a setting from the illustrations?

_____

_____

_____

_____

What is one thing you learn about an event from the illustrations?

_____

_____

_____

 Children analyze and respond to literary texts.

Name _____

DIRECTIONS Write each sentence again using a pronoun.

Mom gets a job.

_____

- -

_____

Bryan likes basketball.

_____

- -

_____

Writing

DIRECTIONS Complete the sentence.

_____

- -

This book is about _____

_____

- -

_____

_____

- -

_____

_____

- -

_____.

Children practice various conventions of standard English. Children write routinely for a range of tasks, purposes, and audiences.

Name _____

DIRECTIONS Add **-ing** to each word. Write it on the line.

1. sell _____

2. look _____

3. fix _____

4. lick _____

Use the words you wrote to finish the sentences.
Write the words on the lines.

5. The man is _____ it.

6. Sam is _____ at the bug.

7. The big cat is _____ the little cat.

8. Jen is _____ cups.

 Children apply grade-level phonics and word analysis skills.

Name _____

DIRECTIONS Choose a word from below and draw it in the box. Then write a sentence using the word.

neatly   shocked

[box for drawing]

_____

- -

_____

DIRECTIONS Complete the sentence.

_____

- -

One way Bryan likes to be perfect is _____

_____

- -

_____

_____

- -

_____

_____

- -

_____

_____

- -

_____.

Children demonstrate contextual understanding of Benchmark Vocabulary. Children read text closely and use text evidence in their written answers.

Name _____

DIRECTIONS Write the sentence again using a pronoun.

Bryan and Tao paint with ink.

_____

_____

DIRECTIONS Draw a picture of something you learned about China. Then write a sentence about your drawing.

_____

_____

_____

 Children practice various conventions of standard English. Children write routinely for a range of tasks, purposes, and audiences.

Name _____

DIRECTIONS Choose a word from below and draw it in the box. Then write a sentence using the word.

promised   exercise

DIRECTIONS Write your answer on the lines below.

What is different about the school in China?

Children demonstrate contextual understanding of Benchmark Vocabulary. Children read text closely and use text evidence in their written answers.

Name _____

DIRECTIONS Circle the right word.

Bryan enjoys (his him he) new school.

Tao and Bryan like (they theirs their) painting.

DIRECTIONS Choose an event or illustration. Write a sentence that tells a fact about it.

_____

_____

_____

_____

_____

Children practice various conventions of standard English. Children write routinely for a range of tasks, purposes, and audiences.

Name _____

DIRECTIONS Choose a word from below and draw it in the box. Then write a sentence using the word.

enjoy   lesson

Write in Response to Reading

DIRECTIONS Complete the sentence.

Bryan enjoys _____

Children demonstrate contextual understanding of Benchmark Vocabulary. Children read text closely and use text evidence in their written answers.

Name _____

DIRECTIONS Circle the words that tell about a noun.

Bryan lives in a tidy house.

The nice boy says hello.

Bryan spills black ink.

Writing

DIRECTIONS Choose an illustration. Think about what it shows. Then write a caption for the illustration.

_____
- -
_____
- -
_____
- -
_____

 Children practice various conventions of standard English. Children write routinely for a range of tasks, purposes, and audiences.

Name _____

DIRECTIONS Circle the word for each picture.

1.

mitt   men   man

2.

bed   bid   bad

3.

pan   pin   pen

4.

tin   tan   ten

5.

jet   jam   jog

6.

not   net   nip

Circle the word that completes each sentence.
Write it on the line.

7. The fat _____ sits on my lap.

    hen   hat

8. I like my big _____ hat.

    rid   red

Children apply grade-level phonics and word analysis skills.

Name _____

DIRECTIONS Choose a word from below and draw it in the box. Then write a sentence using the word.

countries   villages   learn

_____

- -

_____

Write in Response to Reading

DIRECTIONS Write your answer on the lines below.

What is this book all about?

_____

- -

_____

- -

_____

- -

_____

Children demonstrate contextual understanding of Benchmark Vocabulary. Children read text closely and use text evidence in their written answers.

Name _____

DIRECTIONS Add the correct word to each sentence.

at   during

_____
- -
We go to school _____ the day.

_____
- -
I sit _____ my desk.

Writing

DIRECTIONS Look at your illustration. Write a sentence that tells about it.

_____
- -
_____
- -
_____
- -
_____
- -
_____

Children practice various conventions of standard English. Children write routinely for a range of tasks, purposes, and audiences.

Name _____

DIRECTIONS Choose a word from below and draw it in the box. Then write a sentence using the word.

languages   community   weather

```
┌─────────────────────────────────────────┐
│                                         │
│                                         │
│                                         │
│                                         │
│                                         │
│                                         │
└─────────────────────────────────────────┘
```

_____

- -

_____

Write in Response to Reading

What is one thing Maria studies in school?

_____

- -

_____

- -

_____

What is one thing Rosita studies in school?

_____

- -

_____

- -

_____

Children demonstrate contextual understanding of Benchmark Vocabulary. Children read text closely and use text evidence in their written answers.

Name _____

DIRECTIONS Add these missing words to the sentence.

with	to

Children go _____ school _____ friends.

Writing

DIRECTIONS Choose one child to write about. Complete the graphic organizer.

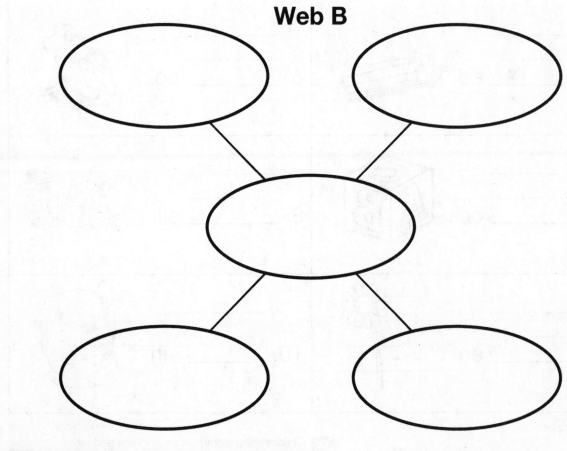

Web B

Children practice various conventions of standard English. Children write routinely for a range of tasks, purposes, and audiences.

Unit 2 • Module B • Lesson 7 • 133

Name _____

DIRECTIONS Pick letters from the box to finish each word.
Write the letters on the line.

bl	cl	cr	dr	fl	fr	gr	sl	sm	st

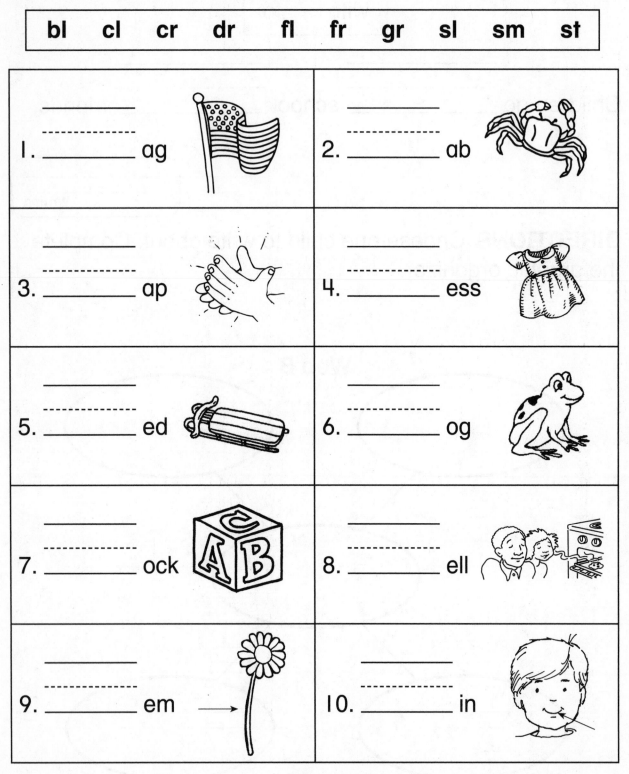

1. _____ ag

2. _____ ab

3. _____ ap

4. _____ ess

5. _____ ed

6. _____ og

7. _____ ock

8. _____ ell

9. _____ em

10. _____ in

Children apply grade-level phonics and word analysis skills.

Name _____

DIRECTIONS Choose a word from below and draw it in the box. Then write a sentence using the word.

native   library   subject

Write in Response to Reading

DIRECTIONS Complete the sentences below.

Levi likes to _____

Daisuke likes _____.

Children demonstrate contextual understanding of Benchmark Vocabulary. Children read text closely and use text evidence in their written answers.

Pizza, Pizza Everywhere

Do you like to eat pizza? I sure do! Pizza is the most interesting food ever!

In America many people like cheese on pizza. I like to eat pepperoni on pizza too. I have eaten pizza all around the world. Not everyone likes the same toppings. I thought some toppings were strange. I found out that they were yummy!

In India, I tried sheep and tofu on pizza. In France, I ate bacon on pizza. In Australia, I tried shrimp and pineapple. In Costa Rica, I had coconut pizza. Are you looking for a new way to eat peas? Then go to Brazil. Many people like peas on their pizza there. I can't wait to try more toppings on pizza!

Think about the toppings the next time you want pizza. Try something new. Enjoy!

Children read text closely to determine what the text says.

Name _____

Look for Clues

On page 136, circle the sentence that tells you the writer thinks pizza is interesting.

Ask Questions

Write two questions you might ask the author about pizza.

_____

- -

_____

- -

_____

- -

_____

Make Your Case

On page 136, draw a box around something you learned from the text that you think is interesting.

Prove It!

If you could try one of the pizza toppings described in the text, which would you try? Tell a partner which topping you picked and why.

Children read text closely to determine what the text says.

DIRECTIONS Fill in the correct verb in the sentence.

play   plays

_____

Friends _____ games together.

Writing

DIRECTIONS Choose one child to write about. Complete the graphic organizer.

Web B

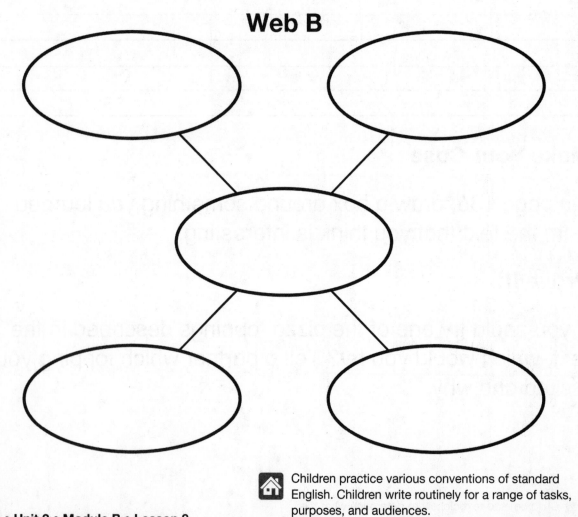

Children practice various conventions of standard English. Children write routinely for a range of tasks, purposes, and audiences.

Name _____

DIRECTIONS Choose a word from below and draw it in the box. Then write a sentence using the word.

ballet   classmates

_____

- -

_____

Write in Response to Reading

DIRECTIONS Complete the sentences.

_____

- -

Olia wants to _____

_____

- -

_____

_____

- -

At recess Sbongile likes to _____

_____

- -

_____

Children demonstrate contextual understanding of Benchmark Vocabulary. Children read text closely and use text evidence in their written answers.

Name _____

DIRECTIONS Circle the words that need capital letters.

Maria lives in kabul, a city in afghanistan.

Levi goes to school on the coast of baffin island.

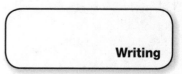

Writing

DIRECTIONS Think about the two children you chose.
Write a sentence that tells how they are alike.

_____

_____

_____

_____

_____

_____

_____

 Children practice various conventions of standard
English. Children write routinely for a range of tasks,
purposes, and audiences.

Name _____

DIRECTIONS Choose a word from below and draw it in the box. Then write a sentence using the word.

blind   diagrams   city

_____

- -

_____

Write in Response to Reading

DIRECTIONS Write your answer on the lines below.

What is one way Samantha and Chavy are alike?

_____

- -

_____

- -

_____

- -

_____

Children demonstrate contextual understanding of Benchmark Vocabulary. Children read text closely and use text evidence in their written answers.

Name _____

DIRECTIONS Circle the words that need capital letters.

olia and sbongile study English.

At recess aseye plays clapping games.

Writing

DIRECTIONS Think about the two children you chose.
Write a sentence that tells how they are different.

_____

- -

_____

- -

_____

_____

- -

_____

_____

- -

_____

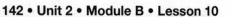

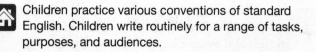
Children practice various conventions of standard
English. Children write routinely for a range of tasks,
purposes, and audiences.

Name _____

DIRECTIONS Say the word for each picture. Write **u** on the line if you hear the **short u** sound.

p<u>u</u>p

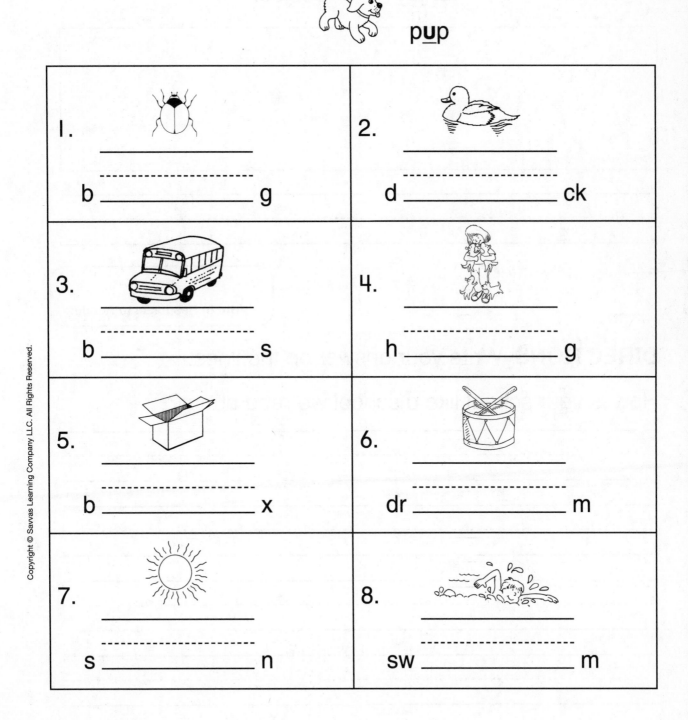

1.

b _____ g

2.

d _____ ck

3.

b _____ s

4.

h _____ g

5.

b _____ x

6.

dr _____ m

7.

s _____ n

8.

sw _____ m

Children apply grade-level phonics and word analysis skills.

Name _____

DIRECTIONS Choose a word from below and draw it in the box. Then write a sentence using the word.

enjoy   subject

```
┌─────────────────────────────────────────┐
│                                         │
│                                         │
│                                         │
│                                         │
└─────────────────────────────────────────┘
```

_____

- -

_____

Write in Response to Reading

DIRECTIONS Write your answer on the lines.

How is your school like a school we read about?

_____

- -

_____

- -

_____

- -

_____

- -

_____

Children demonstrate contextual understanding of Benchmark Vocabulary. Children read text closely and use text evidence in their written answers.

Name _____

DIRECTIONS Draw a picture that shows the main topic of *Going to School.* Then write a sentence that tells the main topic.

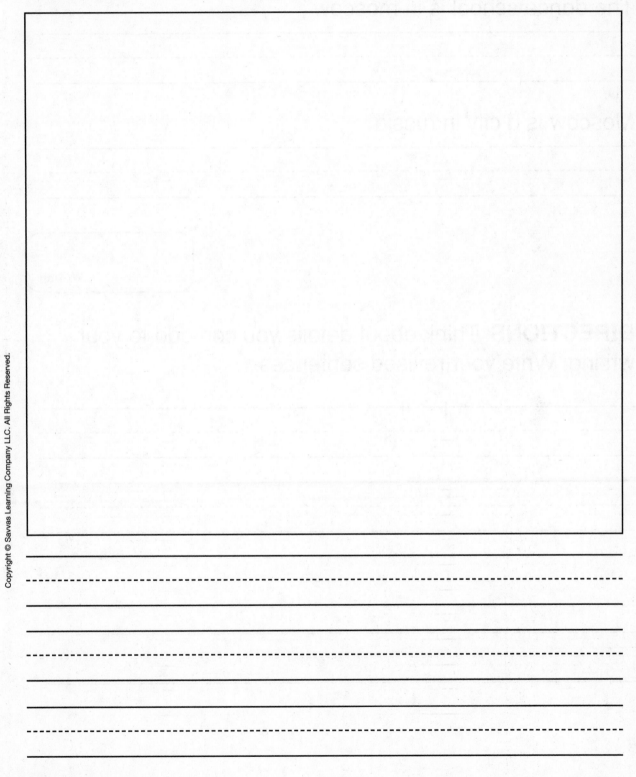

_____

- -

_____

- -

_____

- -

_____

Children analyze and respond to informational texts.

Name _____

DIRECTIONS Write the sentences again. Add capital letters and end marks where needed.

The dance school is in moscow

_____

- -

_____

Moscow is a city in russia

_____

- -

_____

Writing

DIRECTIONS Think about details you can add to your writing. Write your revised sentences.

_____

- -

_____

- -

_____

- -

_____

- -

_____

Children practice various conventions of standard English. Children write routinely for a range of tasks, purposes, and audiences.

Name _____

DIRECTIONS Choose a word from below and draw it in the box. Then write a sentence using the word.

lesson   classmates

Write in Response to Reading

DIRECTIONS Complete the sentence.

I would like to go to school in _____

because _____

Children demonstrate contextual understanding of Benchmark Vocabulary. Children read text closely and use text evidence in their written answers.

Name _____

DIRECTIONS Write a sentence that tells how *Far from Home* and *Going to School* are different. Use examples from the texts.

_____

_____

_____

_____

_____

_____

_____

_____

 Children analyze and respond to literary and informational texts.

Name _____

DIRECTIONS Add the correct word to the sentences.

a   an

_____

Aseye wants to be _____ doctor.

_____

Bryan takes _____ art class.

Writing

DIRECTIONS Copy your sentences on the lines. Use your best handwriting.

_____

_____

_____

_____

_____

Children practice various conventions of standard English. Children write routinely for a range of tasks, purposes, and audiences.

Name _____

DIRECTIONS Say the word for each picture. Circle the letters that finish each word. Write the letters on the line.

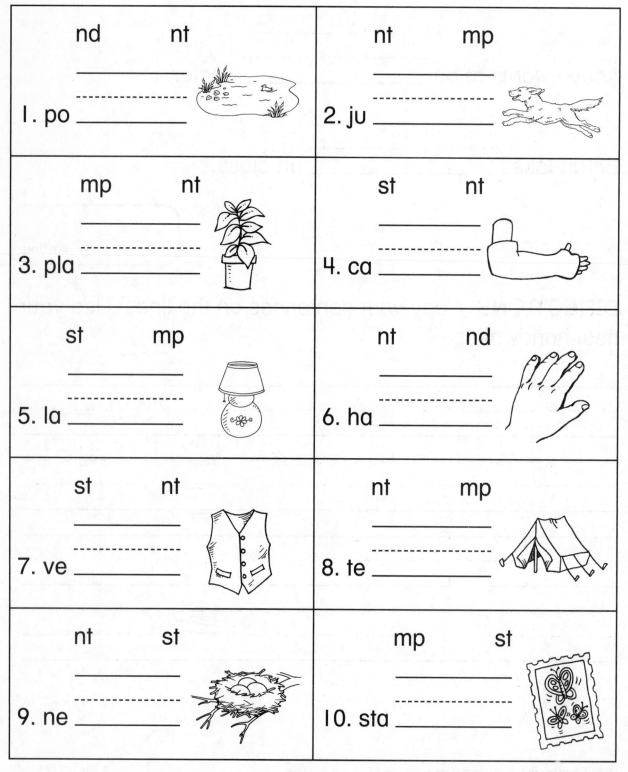

nd   nt

1. po _____

nt   mp

2. ju _____

mp   nt

3. pla _____

st   nt

4. ca _____

st   mp

5. la _____

nt   nd

6. ha _____

st   nt

7. ve _____

nt   mp

8. te _____

nt   st

9. ne _____

mp   st

10. sta _____

 Children apply grade-level phonics and word analysis skills.

Name _____

DIRECTIONS Say the word for each picture.
Write **sh** or **th** to finish the word.

1. _____
   _____ op

2. _____
   fi _____

3. _____
   _____ umb

4. _____
   _____ ell

5. _____
   ba _____

6. _____
   bru _____

Circle a word to finish each sentence. Write the word.

path   math

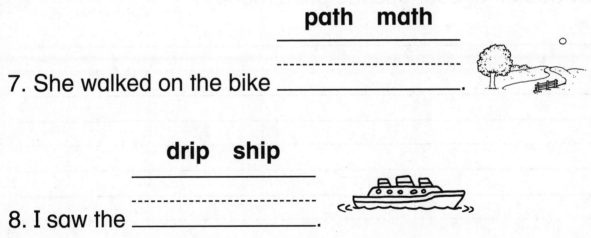

_____
- - - - - - - - - - - - - -

7. She walked on the bike _____ .

drip   ship

_____
- - - - - - - - - - - - - -

8. I saw the _____ .

Children apply grade-level phonics and
word analysis skills.

Name _____

Benchmark Vocabulary

DIRECTIONS Choose a word from below and draw it in the box. Then write a sentence using the word.

trophy money

_____

- -

_____

Write in Response to Reading

DIRECTIONS Write your answer on the lines below.
How does the team use the prize money?

_____

- -

_____

- -

_____

- -

_____

 Children demonstrate contextual understanding of Benchmark Vocabulary. Children read text closely and use text evidence in their written answers.

Name _____

DIRECTIONS Write the correct pronoun on the line.

| He | They |

_____

Carlos had an idea. _____ had an idea.

DIRECTIONS Take notes about the story events on the lines below.

Beginning _____

_____

_____

Middle _____

_____

_____

End _____

_____

Children practice various conventions of standard English. Children write routinely for a range of tasks, purposes, and audiences.

Name _____

DIRECTIONS Choose a word from below and draw it in the box. Then write a sentence using the word.

golden   spend   gasped

_____

- -

_____

Write in Response to Reading

DIRECTIONS Write your answer on the lines below.
What does the team get for winning the soccer tournament?

_____

- -

_____

- -

_____

- -

_____

Children demonstrate contextual understanding of Benchmark Vocabulary. Children read text closely and use text evidence in their written answers.

Name _____

DIRECTIONS Write the correct pronoun on the line.

their	her

_____

Patricia walks home with _____ mom.

DIRECTIONS Write a sentence about the beginning of the story. Then write a sentence about the middle of the story.

Sentence 1: _____

_____

_____

_____

Sentence 2: _____

_____

_____

_____

Children practice various conventions of standard English. Children write routinely for a range of tasks, purposes, and audiences.

Name _____

DIRECTIONS Circle a word to finish each sentence. Write it on the line.

small   smell

_____

1. Look at the _____ cat go up!

tell   tall

_____

2. It is too _____ for us.

call   sell

_____

3. We can _____ Dad.

wall   walk

_____

4. Dad will _____ up.

talk   tell

_____

5. We have a _____ with Dad.

 Children apply grade-level phonics and word analysis skills.

Name _____

DIRECTIONS Draw a picture of the word below in the box. Then write a sentence using the word.

teammates

```
┌─────────────────────────────────────────────┐
│                                             │
│                                             │
│                                             │
│                                             │
│                                             │
│                                             │
└─────────────────────────────────────────────┘
```

_____

- - - - - - - - - - - - - - - - - - -

Write in Response to Reading

DIRECTIONS Complete the sentence.

_____

- - - - - - - - - - - - - - - - - - -

Juan's idea is _____

_____

- - - - - - - - - - - - - - - - - - -

_____

- - - - - - - - - - - - - - - - - - -

_____

- - - - - - - - - - - - - - - - - - -

_____

Children demonstrate contextual understanding of Benchmark Vocabulary. Children read text closely and use text evidence in their written answers.

Name _____

Are You My Kitten?

"Are you my kitten?" Kelly asked. The kitten was black with white paws. Kelly wasn't sure. She saw another kitten. It was gray with a white face. "Are you my kitten?" Kelly still wasn't sure.

Kelly looked at a third kitten. It was gray and black and white all over. It curled up beside its brother and sister in Mrs. Bell's yard. Mrs. Bell's cat had had three kittens.

The kitten touched Kelly's hand with a soft paw. "You are my kitten!" Kelly said. "I will take you home. I will feed you and give you water. I will give you a place to sleep. I will play with you. You are definitely my kitten!"

Children read text closely to determine what the text says.

Name _____

Look for Clues

Circle the words on page 158 that tell what the third kitten looks like.

Ask Questions

On page 158, underline a sentence about taking care of a kitten that you would like to know more about.

Make Your Case

Draw the kitten you would choose. Write words to describe it.

Children read text closely to determine what the text says.

Name _____

DIRECTIONS Circle the words that tell about a noun.

Carlos wants to make a large pool.

The team likes the old uniforms.

A round fountain will get in the way.

Writing

DIRECTIONS Write a sentence about the end of the story.

_____

- -

_____

- -

_____

_____

- -

_____

_____

- -

_____

_____

- -

_____

 Children practice various conventions of standard English. Children write routinely for a range of tasks, purposes, and audiences.

Name _____

DIRECTIONS Choose a word from below and draw it in the box. Then write a sentence using the word.

safe   brave

Write in Response to Reading

DIRECTIONS Write your answer on the lines below. What does Coach Ramos do after the earthquake?

_____

_____

_____

_____

_____

Children demonstrate contextual understanding of Benchmark Vocabulary. Children read text closely and use text evidence in their written answers.

Name _____

DIRECTIONS Circle the word that shows who owns the field.

The (team's / team) field was better than ever.

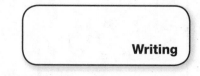

DIRECTIONS Add time or sequence words to your sentences. Write the sentences on the lines below.

_____

_____

_____

_____

_____

_____

_____

_____

_____

_____

 Children practice various conventions of standard English. Children write routinely for a range of tasks, purposes, and audiences.

Name _____

DIRECTIONS Choose a word from below and draw it in the box. Then write a sentence using the word.

damage   zooming

Write in Response to Reading

DIRECTIONS Complete the sentence.

One way the earthquake causes damage is

Children demonstrate contextual understanding of Benchmark Vocabulary. Children read text closely and use text evidence in their written answers.

Name _____

DIRECTIONS Circle the word to use to put the two sentences together.

and   but   or

Patricia saw the ruined field. She had an idea.

Writing

DIRECTIONS Think about details you can add to your sentences. Rewrite the sentences below.

_____

- -

_____

- -

_____

- -

_____

- -

_____

- -

_____

- -

Children practice various conventions of standard English. Children write routinely for a range of tasks, purposes, and audiences.

Name _____

DIRECTIONS Circle the word for each picture.

1.	2.	3.
rake rack	snack snake	frog frame
4.	5.	6.
can cane	cape cap	plane plan

Choose a word to finish each sentence.
Write the word on the line.

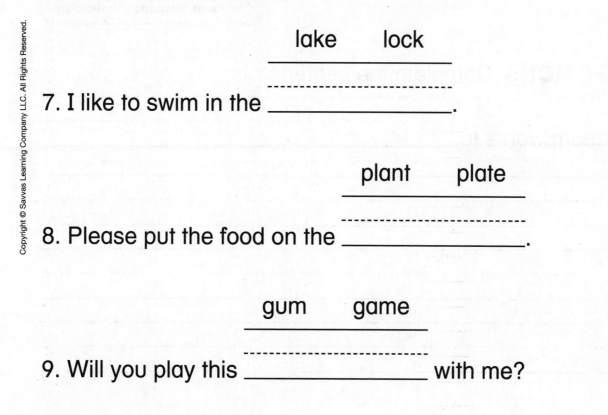

lake   lock

7. I like to swim in the _____.

plant   plate

8. Please put the food on the _____.

gum   game

9. Will you play this _____ with me?

Children apply grade-level phonics and
word analysis skills.

Name _____

DIRECTIONS Choose a word from below and draw it in the box. Then write a sentence using the word.

need   want   position

DIRECTIONS Complete the sentence.

The team wants to _____

Children demonstrate contextual understanding of Benchmark Vocabulary. Children read text closely and use text evidence in their written answers.

Name _____

DIRECTIONS Rewrite the two sentences as one sentence. Use one of the words in the box.

| and | but | or |

The field looked great. Patricia felt proud.

_____

- -

_____

- -

_____

Writing

DIRECTIONS Look at your illustration. Write about what happens.

_____

- -

_____

- -

_____

- -

_____

- -

_____

- -

_____

Children practice various conventions of standard English. Children write routinely for a range of tasks, purposes, and audiences.

Name _____

DIRECTIONS Choose a word from below and draw it in the box. Then write a sentence using the word.

coins   bills

_____

_____

Write in Response to Reading

DIRECTIONS Complete the sentence.

_____

Hunter wants to buy _____

_____

_____

Children demonstrate contextual understanding of Benchmark Vocabulary. Children read text closely and use text evidence in their written answers.

DIRECTIONS Draw a picture that shows the narrator of page 9 in the story. Then write a sentence that tells how you know this is the narrator.

Children analyze and respond to literary texts.

Name _____

DIRECTIONS Rewrite the two sentences as one sentence. Use one of the words in the box.

and	but	or

Hunter wants a skateboard. He doesn't want that one.

_____

- -

_____

- -

_____

Writing

DIRECTIONS Write about the story events in order.

_____

- -

_____

- -

_____

- -

_____

- -

_____

Children practice various conventions of standard English. Children write routinely for a range of tasks, purposes, and audiences.

Name _____

DIRECTIONS Circle the word for each picture.
Write it on the line.

la**ce**

ag**e**

1. face fake _____ ------------ _____	2. rake race _____ ------------ _____	3. wag wage _____ ------------ _____
4. speck space _____ ------------ _____	5. stage stake _____ ------------ _____	6. pace page _____ ------------ _____

Circle the word to finish each sentence. Write the word.

lace   brake

_____

----

7. I tripped on my _____.

page   cage

_____

----

8. My pet bird lives in a _____.

Children apply grade-level phonics and
word analysis skills.

Name _____

DIRECTIONS Choose a word from below and draw it in the box. Then write a sentence using the word.

shiny   bossy

Write in Response to Reading

DIRECTIONS Write your answer on the lines.

Who lives in Hunter's money jar?

 Children demonstrate contextual understanding of Benchmark Vocabulary. Children read text closely and use text evidence in their written answers.

Name _____

DIRECTIONS Find the word with an ending.
Underline the root word. Circle the ending.

The boy counted his money every day.

Writing

DIRECTIONS Think about a time when you made a
choice. Write your idea on the lines.

_____

_____

_____

_____

_____

_____

_____

_____

_____

_____

_____

_____

Children practice various conventions of
standard English. Children write routinely for a
range of tasks, purposes, and audiences.

Name _____

DIRECTIONS Choose a word from below and draw it in the box. Then write a sentence using the word.

count   bank

Write in Response to Reading

DIRECTIONS Write your answer on the lines below.

What does Hunter do with his money?

_____

_____

_____

_____

_____

_____

Children demonstrate contextual understanding of Benchmark Vocabulary. Children read text closely and use text evidence in their written answers.

DIRECTIONS Circle the correct pronoun.

Hunter does not count (our / his) money.

Writing

DIRECTIONS Review your events. Then write about the events below.

_____

- -

_____

- -

_____

- -

_____

- -

_____

- -

_____

- -

_____

Children practice various conventions of standard English. Children write routinely for a range of tasks, purposes, and audiences.

Name _____

DIRECTIONS Choose a word from below and draw it in the box. Then write a sentence using the word.

sell   waste   earn

Write in Response to Reading

DIRECTIONS Write your answer on the lines below.

Why does Scratch think Hunter should keep saving his money?

Children demonstrate contextual understanding of Benchmark Vocabulary. Children read text closely and use text evidence in their written answers.

Name _____

DIRECTIONS Write two words from your web. Then write the meanings of the words below.

Word 1: _____

_____

_____

_____

Word 2: _____

_____

_____

_____

Children analyze and respond to literary texts.

Name _____

DIRECTIONS Add commas to the sentence.

Scratch Hex and Ridge all live in the money jar.

DIRECTIONS Think about how your story ends. Write the ending events below.

_____
_____
_____
_____
_____
_____
_____
_____
_____
_____
_____
_____
_____

Copyright © Savvas Learning Company LLC. All Rights Reserved.

Children practice various conventions of standard English. Children write routinely for a range of tasks, purposes, and audiences.

Name _____

DIRECTIONS Circle the word for each picture.

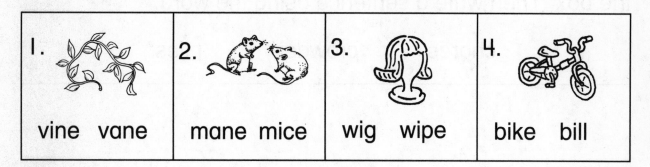

1.	2.	3.	4.
vine vane	mane mice	wig wipe	bike bill

Say the name of each picture.
Write the word on the line.

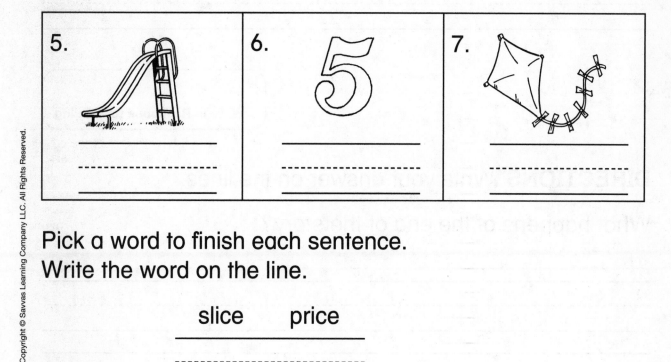

5.	6.	7.

Pick a word to finish each sentence.
Write the word on the line.

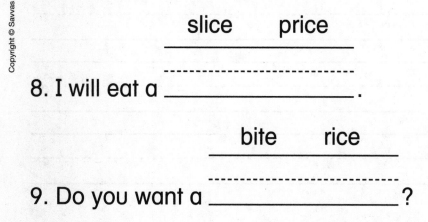

slice   price
_____
- - - - - - - - - - - - - - - - - - -

8. I will eat a _____.

bite   rice
_____
- - - - - - - - - - - - - - - - - - -

9. Do you want a _____?

Children apply grade-level phonics and
word analysis skills.

Name _____

DIRECTIONS Choose a word from below and draw it in the box. Then write a sentence using the word.

chores   crowded   piles

Write in Response to Reading

DIRECTIONS Write your answer on the lines.

What happens at the end of the story?

_____

_____

_____

_____

 Children demonstrate contextual understanding of Benchmark Vocabulary. Children read text closely and use text evidence in their written answers.

Name _____

DIRECTIONS Circle the correct verb.

Hunter (looked / looks / will look) at the skateboard last week.

DIRECTIONS Write your revised story on the lines.

_____

- -

_____

- -

_____

- -

_____

- -

_____

- -

_____

- -

_____

- -

_____

- -

_____

Children practice various conventions of standard English. Children write routinely for a range of tasks, purposes, and audiences.

Name _____

DIRECTIONS Choose a word from below and draw it in the box. Then write a sentence using the word.

ruined   aisles

```



```

_____

- -

_____

Write in Response to Reading

DIRECTIONS Complete the sentences.

The soccer team wants to use their money to

_____

- -

_____

- -

_____

_____

- -

Hunter wants to use his money to _____

_____

- -

_____

Children demonstrate contextual understanding of Benchmark Vocabulary. Children read text closely and use text evidence in their written answers.

Name _____

DIRECTIONS Think about the characters' decisions in *The Winners' Choice* and *Hunter's Money Jar*. Draw pictures to show how their decisions are different.

The Winners' Choice

Hunter's Money Jar

Children analyze and respond to literary texts.

Name _____

DIRECTIONS Circle the correct word to join the sentences.

Hunter could buy the skateboard, (so / or) he could keep saving his money.

DIRECTIONS Think about the mistakes you circled. Write your edited story on the lines.

_____
_____
_____
_____
_____
_____
_____
_____
_____
_____
_____
_____
_____
_____
_____
_____

Children practice various conventions of standard English. Children write routinely for a range of tasks, purposes, and audiences.

Name _____

DIRECTIONS Circle the word for each picture.

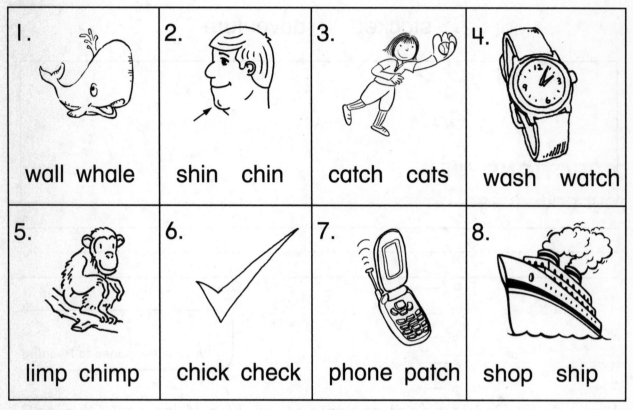

1. wall whale	2. shin chin	3. catch cats	4. wash watch
5. limp chimp	6. chick check	7. phone patch	8. shop ship

Pick a word to finish each sentence.
Write the word on the line.

graph   grass

_____

9. Jim made a mistake on his _____.

what   want

_____

10. He did not know _____ to do.

 Children apply grade-level phonics and
word analysis skills.

Name _____

DIRECTIONS Choose a word from below and draw it in the box. Then write a sentence using the word.

stacked   adventure

```
┌─────────────────────────────────────────────┐
│                                             │
│                                             │
│                                             │
│                                             │
│                                             │
│                                             │
└─────────────────────────────────────────────┘
```

_____

_____

Write in Response to Reading

How does Patricia feel at the end of *The Winners' Choice?*

_____

_____

_____

How does Hunter feel at the end of *Hunter's Money Jar?*

_____

_____

_____

Children demonstrate contextual understanding of Benchmark Vocabulary. Children read text closely and use text evidence in their written answers.

Name _____

Cook Up a Surprise

"Mom," said Amy. "Next week is Ms. Carter's birthday. She likes flowers and dogs and cooking. What surprise can our class make?"

Mom had the best idea. The next day, Amy told everyone. "That's a great idea!" they said.

The next Tuesday was Ms. Carter's birthday. After lunch, Amy raised her hand. Then the whole class said, "Happy birthday, Ms. Carter!"

Luis handed Ms. Carter a big book. On the front was a drawing by Jane. It showed a colorful fruit salad. The title of the book was "Our Best Recipes."

Ms. Carter opened the book. She saw a recipe on each page. There were recipes for many things. The children had gotten recipes from their parents. The recipes were for their favorite foods. They had put them in the book and drawn pictures.

"This is a wonderful surprise," said Ms. Carter. "I'll treasure it forever."

Children read text closely to determine what the text says.

Look for Clues

On page 187, find details that tell what Ms. Carter likes. Underline the details. Then circle the detail you underlined that gave Amy's mom an idea.

Ask Questions

When she opens the book, what might Ms. Carter ask the students? Write a question.

_____

_____

_____

Make Your Case

The students work together to make Ms. Carter a surprise birthday gift. Write a sentence to tell how they feel about Ms. Carter.

_____

_____

_____

Children read text closely to determine what the text says.

Name _____

DIRECTIONS Complete each sentence with one of the words in the box.

this	these

_____

I have _____ coins.

_____

I like _____ skateboard.

DIRECTIONS Think about your story. Write a sentence that tells your favorite part.

_____

_____

_____

_____

_____

_____

_____

Children practice various conventions of standard English. Children write routinely for a range of tasks, purposes, and audiences.

Name _____

DIRECTIONS Write the letters to make a word in each sentence. Then read the story.

_____ _____

R_____s_____ wanted to make soup.

_____ _____

She did not have a **b**_____**n**_____.

_____ _____

So she put a big **st**_____**n**_____ in the pot.

_____ _____

She did not have a **st**_____**v**_____.

_____ _____

She made a fire outside her **h**_____**m**_____.

_____ _____

She hung the pot on a **p**_____**l**_____.

_____ _____

"I **h**_____**p**_____ this will be good," Rose said.

Circle the words that have the same long **o** sound as .

clove	bond	not	poke	stop	spoke
drop	lost	vote	son	color	told

Children apply grade-level phonics and word analysis skills.

Name _____

DIRECTIONS Choose a word below to draw in the box. Then write a sentence using the word.

goods   services

Write in Response to Reading

DIRECTIONS Complete the sentence.

Two goods I use are _____

and _____

Children demonstrate contextual understanding of Benchmark Vocabulary. Children read text closely and use text evidence in their written answers.

Name _____

DIRECTIONS Circle the pronoun. Use it in a sentence.

Taxes pay for services everyone uses.

_____

- -

_____

_____

- -

_____

Writing

Are goods or services more important?
Write your opinion below.

_____
- -
I think _____ are more

_____
- -
important than _____.

Draw a picture of your opinion.

┌─────────────────────────────────────┐
│   │
│   │
│   │
│   │
│   │
│   │
│   │
└─────────────────────────────────────┘

Children practice various conventions of standard English. Children write routinely for a range of tasks, purposes, and audiences.

Name _____

Benchmark Vocabulary

DIRECTIONS Choose a word below to draw in the box. Then write a sentence using the word.

want   need

```
┌─────────────────────────────────────────────┐
│                                             │
│                                             │
│                                             │
│                                             │
│                                             │
│                                             │
└─────────────────────────────────────────────┘
```

_____
- -
_____
_____
- -
_____

Write in Response to Reading

DIRECTIONS Complete the sentences.

_____
- -
Jenna buys a _____.

_____
- -
She is a _____.

(producer/consumer)

Children demonstrate contextual understanding of Benchmark Vocabulary. Children read text closely and use text evidence in their written answers.

Name _____

DIRECTIONS Circle the proper nouns.
Underline the common nouns.

My school is Roosevelt Elementary.

Sesame Avenue is the only street without a stoplight.

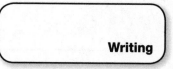

DIRECTIONS Write your supporting reasons below.

_____

I think _____ are more important

_____

because _____

_____

_____

_____

_____

 Children practice various conventions of standard
English. Children write routinely for a range of tasks,
purposes, and audiences.

Name _____

DIRECTIONS Read each sentence.
Write the contraction for the underlined words.

1. "I <u>can not</u> make a nest," said
the little bird.

_____
- - - - - - - - - - - - - - -
_____

2. "<u>I will</u> need help with the sticks,"
said the little bird.

_____
- - - - - - - - - - - - - - -
_____

3. "I <u>do not</u> think I can help," said
the frog.

_____
- - - - - - - - - - - - - - -
_____

4. "<u>You will</u> need a big bird to help you,"
said the frog.

_____
- - - - - - - - - - - - - - -
_____

5. "<u>I am</u> a big bird! I can help," said
the big bird.

_____
- - - - - - - - - - - - - - -
_____

Children apply grade-level phonics and word
analysis skills.

Name _____

DIRECTIONS Choose a word below to draw in the box. Then write a sentence using the word.

collects   taxes

_____
_____
_____
_____

Write in Response to Reading

DIRECTIONS Complete the sentence.

_____

The government collects _____

List two services the taxes pay for.

_____
_____
_____
_____

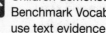
Children demonstrate contextual understanding of Benchmark Vocabulary. Children read text closely and use text evidence in their written answers.

Name _____

DIRECTIONS Circle the word that has an **-s** ending added to the root word.

drops   bass   gross

DIRECTIONS Write your opinion about one of the sections in the text. Then write a reason that supports your opinion.

My Opinion: _____

My Reason: _____

Children practice various conventions of standard English. Children write routinely for a range of tasks, purposes, and audiences.

Name _____

Benchmark Vocabulary

DIRECTIONS Choose a word below to draw in the box.
Then write a sentence using the word.

supermarket   necessary   shoppers

[drawing box]

_____

- -

_____

- -

_____

Write in Response to Reading

DIRECTIONS Complete the sentence.

_____

- -

A supermarket has _____

_____

- -

and _____

_____

- -

_____

Children demonstrate contextual understanding of
Benchmark Vocabulary. Children read text closely and
use text evidence in their written answers.

Name _____

DIRECTIONS Circle the word that makes sense.

That truck is (big / bigger) than this truck.

Today is the (warmer / warmest) day of the year!

Writing

DIRECTIONS List opinion words about a food you like or dislike. Draw a picture of the food.

_____

Opinion words: _____

_____

_____

_____

Children practice various conventions of standard English. Children write routinely for a range of tasks, purposes, and audiences.

Name _____

DIRECTIONS Choose a word below to draw in the box. Then write a sentence using the word.

producers   farmers   decisions

_____

- -

_____

- -

_____

Write in Response to Reading

DIRECTIONS Complete the sentence.

_____

- -

If I had a farm, I would grow _____

_____

- -

because _____

_____

- -

_____

_____

- -

Children demonstrate contextual understanding of Benchmark Vocabulary. Children read text closely and use text evidence in their written answers.

Name _____

DIRECTIONS Draw a picture of a producer and consumer from *Goods and Services.* Label your drawing.

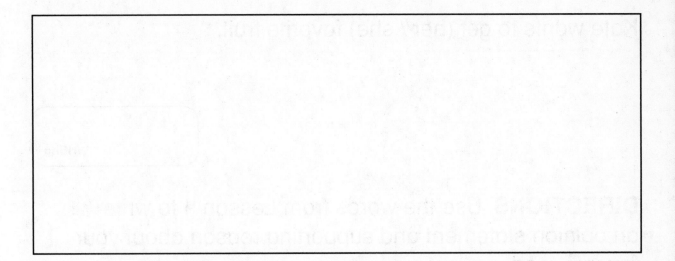

Draw a picture of a producer and consumer from *Supermarket.* Label your drawing.

Discuss with a partner how your pictures are similar and different.

Children analyze and respond to informational text.

DIRECTIONS Circle the word that makes sense.

Put the food in (your / you) cart.

Kate wants to get (her / she) favorite fruit.

Writing

DIRECTIONS Use the words from Lesson 4 to write an opinion statement and supporting reason about your favorite food.

_____

- -

_____

_____

- -

_____

_____

- -

_____

_____

- -

_____

_____

- -

_____

Children practice various conventions of standard English. Children write routinely for a range of tasks, purposes, and audiences.

Name _____

DIRECTIONS Circle the word for each picture.

c<u>u</u>be

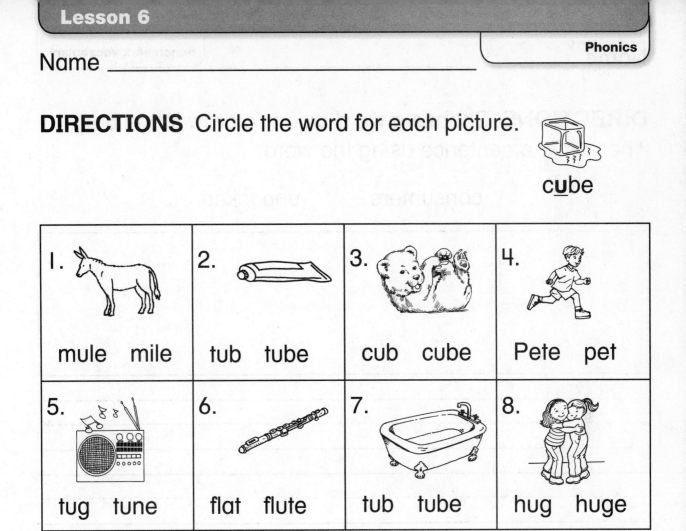

1. mule mile	2. tub tube	3. cub cube	4. Pete pet
5. tug tune	6. flat flute	7. tub tube	8. hug huge

Find the word that has the same **long u** sound as .

Circle the letter.

9. **A.** rut
   B. rid
   C. rule

10. **A.** cut
    B. cute
    C. cup

Children apply grade-level phonics and word analysis skills.

Name _____

DIRECTIONS Choose a word below to draw in the box. Then write a sentence using the word.

consumers   unpacked

Write in Response to Reading

DIRECTIONS Complete the sentence.

Goods and services are alike because they both are

Children demonstrate contextual understanding of Benchmark Vocabulary. Children read text closely and use text evidence in their written answers.

Name _____

DIRECTIONS Circle the word that makes sense.

Nan (was / were) a customer at the store.

Writing

DIRECTIONS Provide a concluding statement for your opinion from Lesson 5.

_____
- -
_____
- -
_____
- -
_____
- -
_____
- -
_____
- -
_____

Children practice various conventions of standard English. Children write routinely for a range of tasks, purposes, and audiences.

Name _____

DIRECTIONS Draw a picture of the word.
Write a sentence using the word.

earn

_____

_____

Write in Response to Reading

What do producers and consumers do?

_____

Producers _____

_____

_____

Consumers _____

_____

_____

Children demonstrate contextual understanding of
Benchmark Vocabulary. Children read text closely and
use text evidence in their written answers.

Name _____

DIRECTIONS Circle the word that makes sense.

My mom (buy / buys) candy as a treat.

Writing

DIRECTIONS Choose a topic for your opinion piece.
List three topics related to shopping:

1. _____

2. _____

3. _____

What topic will you write about?

_____

_____

_____

Children practice various conventions of standard English. Children write routinely for a range of tasks, purposes, and audiences.

Name _____

DIRECTIONS Pick a word from the box to finish each sentence. Add **-ed** to each word. Write it on the line.

call	walk	sniff	jump	rest

_____

1. They _____ rope together.

_____

2. Pam _____ June.

_____

3. They _____ to the park.

_____

4. They _____ in the shade.

_____

5. They _____ the flowers.

Children apply grade-level phonics and word analysis skills.

Lesson 8

Benchmark Vocabulary

Name _____

DIRECTIONS Draw the word in the box. Then write a sentence using the word.

choices

_____

_____

_____

> **Write in Response to Reading**

What do producers and consumers do with money?

_____

Producers _____

_____

_____

Consumers _____

_____

_____

Children demonstrate contextual understanding of Benchmark Vocabulary. Children read text closely and use text evidence in their written answers.

Unit 3 • Module B • Lesson 8 • 209

Help Yourself and Others

Have you cleaned out your toy chest or closet lately? You probably have some clothes that are too small. You have toys that you don't play with. Don't keep old clothes and toys. Give them to someone who needs them.

Yesterday I cleaned my closet. I tried on a sweater. Did it shrink? No, I had grown. After I sorted clothes, I looked through toys. There were three games, four stuffed animals, and a train set that I never play with.

Soon I had a pile of clothes and toys. My mom and I put them in bags and took them into town. We put them in a huge bin. Someone will collect the things. Then they'll give them to people who need them.

Giving away unneeded clothes and toys is a great idea. You help others. You recycle valuable things. Everyone should clean out, give away, and recycle!

 Children read text closely to determine what the text says.

Name _____

Look for Clues

On page 210, circle words that tell what the family does to help others.

Ask Questions

What questions do you want to ask the writer?

Make Your Case

Circle words the writer wants us to think about.

Make Your Case: Extend Your Ideas

Write a sentence that tells why it is important to give away what we no longer need.

_____

_____

_____

_____

_____

🏠 Children read text closely and use text evidence in their written answers.

Name _____

DIRECTIONS Circle the preposition.

She went to Florida during the winter.

The campground is beyond the trees.

DIRECTIONS Choose one topic from Lesson 7.
Write an opinion statement.

_____
_____
Topic: _____
_____
_____

Opinion Statement

_____
_____
_____
_____
_____
_____
_____
_____

Children practice various conventions of standard English. Children write routinely for a range of tasks, purposes, and audiences.

Name _____

DIRECTIONS Choose a word to draw in the box. Then write a sentence using the word.

inventory   spoiled

_____

_____

_____

Write in Response to Reading

What happens at the checkout counter?

_____

_____

_____

_____

Children demonstrate contextual understanding of Benchmark Vocabulary. Children read text closely and use text evidence in their written answers.

Unit 3 • Module B • Lesson 9 • 213

Name _____

DIRECTIONS Write an end mark at the end of each sentence.

Wow! Look at all that candy

Watch out

Writing

DIRECTIONS Write a supporting sentence for your opinion from Lesson 8.

_____

- -

_____

_____

- -

_____

_____

- -

_____

_____

- -

_____

_____

- -

_____

_____

- -

_____

_____

- -

_____

Children practice various conventions of standard English. Children write routinely for a range of tasks, purposes, and audiences.

Name _____

DIRECTIONS Choose a word to draw in the box. Then write a sentence using the word.

average   celebrate

Write in Response to Reading

DIRECTIONS Complete the sentence.

Supermarkets are important because _____

Children demonstrate contextual understanding of Benchmark Vocabulary. Children read text closely and use text evidence in their written answers.

Name _____

DIRECTIONS Circle the words that make sense.

Give (to / two / too) sticks of gum (to / two / too) Jen.

DIRECTIONS Rewrite your opinion statement from Lesson 9 to include a concluding sentence.

_____

_____

_____

_____

_____

_____

_____

_____

_____

_____

_____

_____

Children practice various conventions of standard English. Children write routinely for a range of tasks, purposes, and audiences.

Name _____

DIRECTIONS Help the bee get home. Read each word.
Draw a line that goes past only the **long e** words.
Write the **long e** words on the line.

1. _____

2. _____

3. _____

4. _____

5. _____

6. _____

7. _____

8. _____

Children apply grade-level phonics and word
analysis skills.

Name _____

DIRECTIONS Choose a word to draw in the box.
Then write a sentence using the word.

goods   services   shoppers

_____

_____

_____

Write in Response to Reading

Which small store on page 55 in *Supermarket* would you
like to visit? _____

I would like to visit _____

_____ because

_____

_____

_____

Children demonstrate contextual understanding of
Benchmark Vocabulary. Children read text closely and
use text evidence in their written answers.

Name _____

DIRECTIONS Circle the word that has more than one meaning. Draw a picture of both meanings in the box. Write a sentence for each drawing.

The supermarket has row after row of colors, shapes, and words that shout.

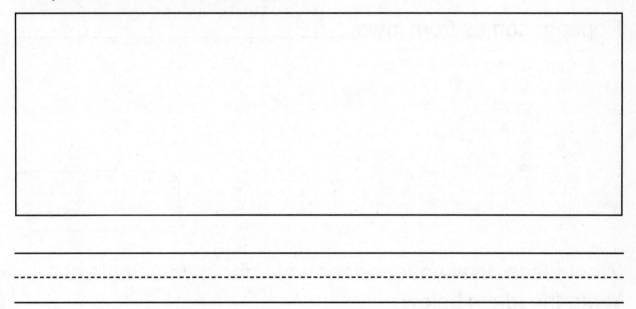

_____

_____

_____

_____

_____

_____

_____

_____

_____

Children analyze and respond to literary and informational text.

Name _____

DIRECTIONS Circle the word that should begin with a capital letter. Then write those words on the lines.

Oranges come from florida. _____

_____

Popcorn comes from iowa. _____

What ideas does your partner have about your writing? Write the ideas below.

_____

_____

_____

_____

_____

_____

_____

Children practice various conventions of standard English. Children write routinely for a range of tasks, purposes, and audiences.

Name _____

DIRECTIONS Choose a word to draw in the box. Write a sentence using the word.

producers   consumers   decisions

_____

- -

_____

- -

_____

Write in Response to Reading

What are your favorite things to buy at the supermarket? Write your answer as a complete sentence.

_____

- -

_____

- -

_____

- -

_____

- -

Children demonstrate contextual understanding of Benchmark Vocabulary. Children read text closely and use text evidence in their written answers.

DIRECTIONS Read page 56. Look at the picture. What information do you get from the words? What information do you get from the picture? Draw or write it in the chart.

Words	Picture

Children analyze and respond to literary and informational text.

Name _____

DIRECTIONS Circle the action word.
Write the action word to show it happened in the past.

_____

Farmers pick fruit. _____

_____

They pack fruit in boxes. _____

Writing

DIRECTIONS Write your opinion as a blog post.

_____
_____
_____
_____
_____
_____
_____
_____
_____
_____
_____
_____
_____
_____

Children practice various conventions of
standard English. Children write routinely for a
range of tasks, purposes, and audiences.

Name _____

DIRECTIONS Circle the word for each picture.

ki**tt**en

1. ramp rabbit	2. button brake	3. dinner dent	4. base basket
5. helmet hello	6. mitten mute	7. mask muffin	8. wall walnut

Draw a picture for each word.

9. napkin

10. picnic

Children apply grade-level phonics and word analysis skills.

Name _____

DIRECTIONS Circle the word for each picture.

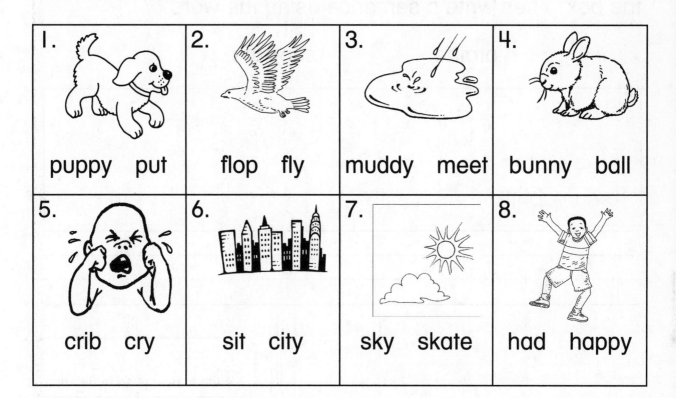

1. puppy put	2. flop fly	3. muddy meet	4. bunny ball
5. crib cry	6. sit city	7. sky skate	8. had happy

Circle the word to finish each sentence. Write it on the line.

_____

----

9. I didn't eat dinner, and I am very _____.

hungry   **money**

10. I jumped in the puddle, so my feet

----

are not _____.

dry   **drip**

Children apply grade-level phonics and word analysis skills.

Name _____

DIRECTIONS Choose a word from below and draw it in the box. Then write a sentence using the word.

prairie   saplings

_____

- -

_____

Write in Response to Reading

DIRECTIONS Write your answer on the lines.

What is Arbor Day?

_____

- -

_____

_____

- -

_____

_____

- -

_____

Children demonstrate contextual understanding of Benchmark Vocabulary. Children read text closely and use text evidence in their written answers.

Name _____

DIRECTIONS Circle the verb to complete the sentence.

Today Arbor Day (is / was) a holiday.

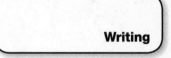

DIRECTIONS Draw a picture of Katie. Then write a sentence about her.

Children practice various conventions of standard English.
Children write routinely for a range of tasks, purposes, and audiences.

Name _____

DIRECTIONS Choose a word from below and draw it in the box. Then write a sentence using the word.

lumber   logs   shade

_____

_____

Write in Response to Reading

DIRECTIONS Draw a picture to show what the train brings. Then write a sentence on the lines below that tells one thing it brings.

_____

_____

_____

_____

Children demonstrate contextual understanding of Benchmark Vocabulary. Children read text closely and use text evidence in their written answers.

Name _____

DIRECTIONS Circle the word that tells about a noun.

The stores have big windows.

The tall trees give us shade.

DIRECTIONS Draw a picture of the setting of *Arbor Day Square.* Then write a sentence to tell about the setting.

Children practice various conventions of standard English. Children write routinely for a range of tasks, purposes, and audiences.

Name _____

DIRECTIONS Circle a word to finish each sentence.
Write it on the line.

He   Hi
_____
- - - - - - - - - - - - - - - -
1. "_____," Luke said.

Hi   He
_____
- - - - - - - - - - - - - - - -
2. _____ is little.

No   Nod
_____
- - - - - - - - - - - - - - - -
3. _____ one can see him.

so   see
_____
- - - - - - - - - - - - - - - -
4. She is _____ big.

bed   be
_____
- - - - - - - - - - - - - - - -
5. He will grow to _____ big too.

Children apply grade-level phonics and word
analysis skills.

Name _____

DIRECTIONS Choose a word from below and draw it in the box. Then write a sentence using the word.

town   skips   unload

Write in Response to Reading

DIRECTIONS Write your answer on the lines.

Why do the people collect money in a basket?

Children demonstrate contextual understanding of Benchmark Vocabulary. Children read text closely and use text evidence in their written answers.

Name _____

A Mentor for James

James loved school. He loved reading and writing. He loved playing soccer outside. But sometimes James didn't like math. Sometimes adding and subtracting was hard.

"Come after school on Tuesday," Ms. Garcia said. "A student called a mentor will help you."

On Tuesday, James worried about staying after school. Who would his mentor be?

After school, James walked to Room 111. He saw other first graders working quietly with older students. A girl walked up.

"Hi, James," she said. "I'm Maria, and I'm in fifth grade. I'll help you with math." They sat down, and James showed Maria his math workbook. They talked about each math problem. Maria was very patient.

Maria said their time was up. James was amazed. He had done all his math problems.

"Thanks, Maria. May I come back next week?" James asked.

"Sure," Maria said. "And will you help me with my soccer sometime?"

Children read text closely to determine what the text says.

Name _____

Look for Clues

Draw a box around the word that tells how James feels after he meets Maria. Underline the sentence that tells why James feels that way.

Ask Questions

Write a question you might ask Maria about being a mentor.

_____

_____

_____

Make Your Case

Retell the story to a partner. Circle a name to finish the sentence: I will tell the story as <u>James   Maria</u>.
Write the first sentence of your retelling. Use "I."

_____

_____

_____

_____

_____

Children read text closely to determine what the text says.

Name _____

DIRECTIONS Circle the verbs to finish the sentences.

Katie and Papa (went / go) to the meeting last week.

The train (come / came) yesterday.

DIRECTIONS Think about the family tradition your story will be about. Write to tell about the tradition.

_____

- -

_____

- -

_____

- -

_____

- -

_____

- -

_____

Children practice various conventions of standard English. Children write routinely for a range of tasks, purposes, and audiences.

Name _____

DIRECTIONS Choose a word from below and draw it in the box. Then write a sentence using the word.

parade   soil   neighbors

_____

_____

Write in Response to Reading

DIRECTIONS Complete the sentence with two things the people plant.

_____

The people plant _____
_____

_____

_____

_____

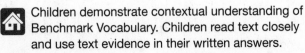

Children demonstrate contextual understanding of Benchmark Vocabulary. Children read text closely and use text evidence in their written answers.

Name _____

DIRECTIONS Write the verb to complete the sentence.

hug   hugs

_____

Papa _____ Katie.

Writing

DIRECTIONS Write your story.

_____
_____
_____
_____
_____
_____
_____
_____
_____
_____
_____

Children practice various conventions of standard English. Children write routinely for a range of tasks, purposes, and audiences.

Name _____

DIRECTIONS Choose a word from below and draw it in the box. Then write a sentence using the word.

holiday   rakes

Write in Response to Reading

DIRECTIONS Write your answer on the lines.
Why do the people want trees?

_____

_____
_____

_____
_____

_____
_____

_____

Children demonstrate contextual understanding of Benchmark Vocabulary. Children read text closely and use text evidence in their written answers.

Unit 4 • Module A • Lesson 5 • 237

Name _____

DIRECTIONS Rewrite the sentence. Add a detail.

The people gather to plant trees.

_____

- -

_____

_____

- -

_____

Writing

DIRECTIONS Think about details you can add to your story. Rewrite the story below.

_____

- -

_____

- -

_____

_____

- -

_____

_____

- -

_____

_____

- -

_____

Children practice various conventions of standard English. Children write routinely for a range of tasks, purposes, and audiences.

Name _____

DIRECTIONS Circle the word for each picture.

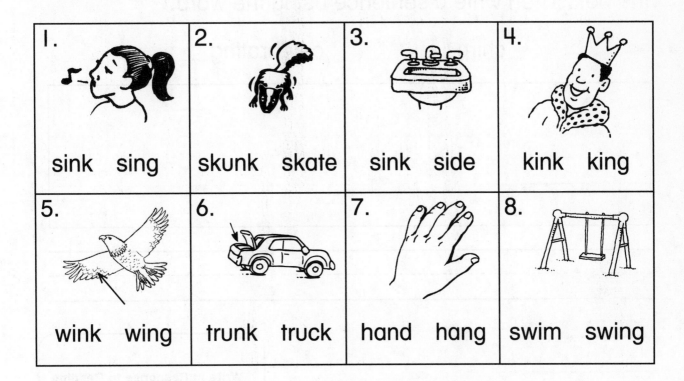

1. sink sing	2. skunk skate	3. sink side	4. kink king
5. wink wing	6. trunk truck	7. hand hang	8. swim swing

Write the letters **ng** or **nk** to finish the words
for each sentence.

9. Please bri_____ me a dri_____.

10. Tha_____ you for the pretty ri_____.

 Children apply grade-level phonics and word
analysis skills.

Name _____

DIRECTIONS Choose a word from below and draw it in the box. Then write a sentence using the word.

chirp   celebrating

_____

- -

_____

Write in Response to Reading

DIRECTIONS Draw what the Square looks like now. Then write a sentence on the lines below to tell one way the Square has changed.

_____

- -

_____

_____

- -

_____

_____

- -

_____

_____

- -

_____

Children demonstrate contextual understanding of Benchmark Vocabulary. Children read text closely and use text evidence in their written answers.

Name _____

DIRECTIONS Write the verb to complete the sentence.

watered   water   will water

_____

They _____ the trees tomorrow.

Writing

DIRECTIONS Think about time and sequence words you can add to your story. Rewrite the story below.

_____

_____

_____

_____

_____

_____

_____

_____

_____

_____

_____

_____

_____

_____

Children practice various conventions of standard English. Children write routinely for a range of tasks, purposes, and audiences.

Name _____

DIRECTIONS Choose a word from below and draw it in the box. Then write a sentence using the word.

huge   success

┌───┐
│   │
│   │
│   │
│   │
│   │
│   │
└───┘

_____

_____

_____

Write in Response to Reading

DIRECTIONS Complete the sentence with two places where Arbor Day is celebrated.

Arbor Day is celebrated in _____

_____

_____

_____

_____

Children demonstrate contextual understanding of Benchmark Vocabulary. Children read text closely and use text evidence in their written answers.

Name _____

DIRECTIONS Write a sentence that tells how the Author's Note and story in *Arbor Day Square* are different.

_____

- -

_____

- -

_____

- -

_____

- -

_____

- -

_____

- -

_____

- -

_____

- -

_____

- -

_____

- -

Children analyze and respond to literary and informational texts.

Name _____

DIRECTIONS Circle the words that need capital letters.

katie and megan anne look at the trees.

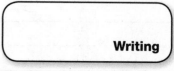

DIRECTIONS Think about the mistakes you circled. Write your edited story on the lines.

_____
- -
_____
_____
- -
_____
_____
- -
_____
_____
- -
_____
_____
- -
_____
_____
- -
_____

Children practice various conventions of standard English. Children write routinely for a range of tasks, purposes, and audiences.

Name _____

DIRECTIONS Pick a word from the box to finish each compound word. Write it on the line. Draw a line to the picture it matches.

| ball   cakes   pole   set |

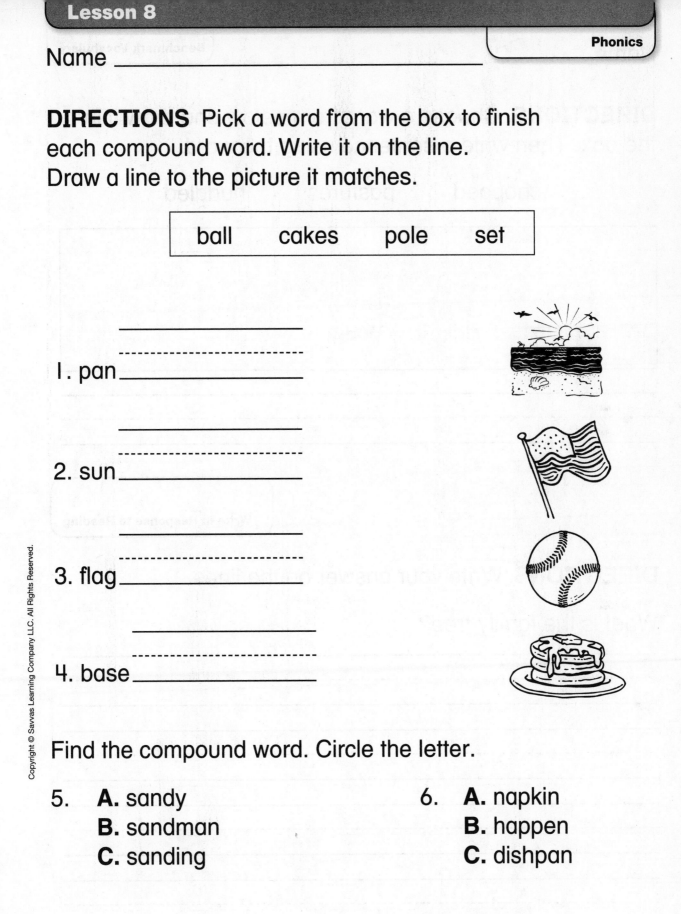

1. pan _____

2. sun _____

3. flag _____

4. base _____

Find the compound word. Circle the letter.

5.   **A.** sandy
     B. sandman
     C. sanding

6.   **A.** napkin
     B. happen
     C. dishpan

Children apply grade-level phonics and word analysis skills.

Name _____

DIRECTIONS Choose a word from below and draw it in the box. Then write a sentence using the word.

chopped   pastures   huddled

_____

- -

_____

Write in Response to Reading

DIRECTIONS Write your answer on the lines.

What is the family tree?

_____

- -

_____

- -

_____

- -

_____

- -

_____

Name _____

DIRECTIONS Write the past tense form of the verb **stop**.

_____

The boy _____ the workers.

Writing

DIRECTIONS Think about what might happen after *The Family Tree* ends. Write a story about what happens.

_____

_____

_____

_____

_____

_____

_____

_____

_____

_____

_____

_____

_____

_____

Children practice various conventions of standard English. Children write routinely for a range of tasks, purposes, and audiences.

Name _____

DIRECTIONS Draw a picture of the word below in the box. Then write a sentence using the word.

years

```
┌─────────────────────────────────┐
│                                 │
│                                 │
│                                 │
│                                 │
│                                 │
└─────────────────────────────────┘
```

_____

- -

_____

Write in Response to Reading

DIRECTIONS Write your answer on the lines.

Why does the man leave one tree standing?

_____

- -

_____

- -

_____

- -

_____

Children demonstrate contextual understanding of Benchmark Vocabulary. Children read text closely and use text evidence in their written answers.

Name _____

DIRECTIONS Write a question you have about the story. Then write the answer to your question.

_____

Question: _____

_____

_____

_____

_____

_____

Answer: _____

_____

_____

_____

_____

_____

Children analyze and respond to literary texts.

Name _____

DIRECTIONS Underline the verb in the sentence. Then circle when the action happens.

The man returned with his wife.   past now future

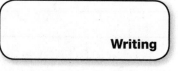

Writing

DIRECTIONS Think about changes you can make to your story. Rewrite your story below.

_____

_____

_____

_____

_____

_____

_____

_____

_____

_____

Children practice various conventions of standard English. Children write routinely for a range of tasks, purposes, and audiences.

Name _____

DIRECTIONS Choose a word from below and draw it in the box. Then write a sentence using the word.

widen   protested

```



```

_____

- -

_____

Write in Response to Reading

DIRECTIONS Write your answer on the lines.

Why does the boy stand in front of the tree?

_____

- -

_____

- -

_____

_____

- -

_____

_____

- -

_____

Children demonstrate contextual understanding of Benchmark Vocabulary. Children read text closely and use text evidence in their written answers.

Name _____

DIRECTIONS Circle the verb to finish the sentence.

Yesterday the boy (is / was) sad.

DIRECTIONS Think about details you can add to your event. Rewrite the event below.

_____

- -

_____

- -

_____

- -

_____

- -

_____

- -

_____

- -

_____

Children practice various conventions of standard English. Children write routinely for a range of tasks, purposes, and audiences.

Name _____

DIRECTIONS Add the ending.
Write the new word on the line.

Word	Ending	New Word
1. mix	+ -es	
2. brush	+ -es	
3. glass	+ -es	
4. catch	+ -es	
5. dress	+ -es	
6. bus	+ -es	
7. dish	+ -es	
8. fox	+ -es	
9. pass	+ -es	
10. patch	+ -es	

Children apply grade-level phonics and word analysis skills.

Name _____

Benchmark Vocabulary

DIRECTIONS Draw a picture of the word below in the box. Then write a sentence using the word.

assistance

_____

- -

_____

Write in Response to Reading

DIRECTIONS Write your answer on the lines.

What is the workers' new plan?

_____

- -

_____

- -

_____

- -

_____

- -

_____

Children demonstrate contextual understanding of Benchmark Vocabulary. Children read text closely and use text evidence in their written answers.

Name _____

DIRECTIONS Write your answers on the lines.

What is the big idea of the story?

_____

- -

_____

- -

_____

- -

_____

- -

What is one thing you learn about the big idea from the details in the story?

_____

- -

_____

- -

_____

- -

_____

- -

_____

- -

Children analyze and respond to literary texts.

Name _____

DIRECTIONS Fill in the right pronoun for the underlined noun.

The young <u>man</u> chopped down trees.

_____

_____ built a house.

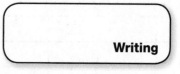

Writing

DIRECTIONS Check the items your partner did in the story. Write one change your partner should make.

Revising Checklist

☐ The events are in the right order.

☐ The writer uses time-order words.

☐ The events focus on one topic.

☐ Details tell about each event.

A change I think the writer should make:

_____

- -

_____

- -

_____

- -

_____

Children practice various conventions of standard English. Children write routinely for a range of tasks, purposes, and audiences.

Benchmark Vocabulary

Name _____

DIRECTIONS Choose a word from below and draw it in the box. Then write a sentence using the word.

special   alone

_____

- -

_____

Write in Response to Reading

What is one thing that Katie does?

_____

- -

_____

- -

_____

What is one thing that the boy does?

_____

- -

_____

- -

_____

Children demonstrate contextual understanding of Benchmark Vocabulary. Children read text closely and use text evidence in their written answers.

Name _____

DIRECTIONS Fill in the right pronoun for the underlined noun.

The <u>neighbors</u> dance. _____

The moon shines on _____.

Writing

DIRECTIONS Write an ending for your story.

_____

_____

_____

_____

_____

_____

_____

_____

_____

_____

_____

_____

 Children practice various conventions of standard English. Children write routinely for a range of tasks, purposes, and audiences.

Name _____

DIRECTIONS Circle the word for each picture.

st<u>or</u>m

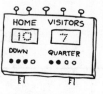

sc<u>ore</u>

1. fork flick	2. hen horn	3. core conk	4. store stock
5. con corn	6. shorts shots	7. port pot	8. thorn tone

Find the word that has the same middle sound as .
Circle the letter.

9. **A.** porch
    B. poke
    C. pole

10. **A.** such
    B. shut
    C. shore

Children apply grade-level phonics and word analysis skills.

Name _____

DIRECTIONS Draw a picture of the word below in the box. Then write a sentence using the word.

celebrating

_____

- -

_____

Write in Response to Reading

DIRECTIONS Complete the sentences.

One thing I learned in *Arbor Day Square* is

_____

- -

_____

One thing I learned in *The Family Tree* is

_____

- -

_____

Children demonstrate contextual understanding of Benchmark Vocabulary. Children read text closely and use text evidence in their written answers.

Name _____

Let's Build a Park!

Luis and his family live in a house in the city. They have a small yard. There is no place to play ball or swing or slide. So Luis's family and their neighbors built a park. Here's how.

First, they picked a spot. Near Luis's house was a big, empty lot with concrete and weeds. It would be perfect! Next, the neighbors planned the park. Would it have a ball field and a playground? Would it have picnic tables?

Next, the neighbors went to their city leaders. They talked about their plan. The leaders voted yes. They gave them some money. The neighbors raised money too. They had a block party and sold food.

The neighbors built the park. Mr. Nuñez planted grass. Mr. Johnson built tables.

Mrs. Parker's company donated swings and slides.

Now Luis's neighborhood has a great place to play, rest, and eat.

 Children read text closely to determine what the text says.

Name _____

Look for Clues
Circle words that tell what the neighbors planted, built, and donated for the new park.

Ask Questions
Write two questions that city leaders might ask the neighbors.

_____

- -

_____

- -

_____

- -

_____

- -

_____

Ask Questions: Extend Your Ideas
Suppose the leaders ask the neighbors why they need a park. Underline the sentence in the story that will answer the question.

Make Your Case
Circle the word that tells what neighbors can do on the swings and slides. Underline the word that tells what they can do on the grass. Box the word that tells what neighbors can do at the tables.

 Children read text closely to determine what the text says.

Name _____

DIRECTIONS Write the sentences.
Use pronouns for the underlined nouns.

<u>Katie</u> spreads a blanket.

_____
- -
_____

<u>The neighbors</u> have a picnic.

_____
- -
_____

Writing

DIRECTIONS How will you publish and share your story?
Write your plan.

_____
- -
_____
- -
_____
_____
- -
_____
_____
- -
_____

Children practice various conventions of standard English. Children write routinely for a range of tasks, purposes, and audiences.

Name _____

DIRECTIONS Add **-ed** and **-ing** to each word.
Write the new words on the lines.

		Add -ed	**Add -ing**
1.	nap		
2.	pat		
3.	nod		
4.	jog		
5.	wag		
6.	stop		
7.	pet		
8.	drop		
9.	clap		
10.	plan		

Children apply grade-level phonics and word analysis skills.

Name _____

DIRECTIONS Choose a word from below and draw it in the box. Then write a sentence using the word.

sunlight   warmth

Write in Response to Reading

DIRECTIONS Write your answer on the lines.

What do apple seeds need?

Children demonstrate contextual understanding of Benchmark Vocabulary. Children read text closely and use text evidence in their written answers.

Name _____

DIRECTIONS Circle the nouns that name more than one.

trunk   trunks   blossom   blossoms

Writing

DIRECTIONS Name the topic of *The Life Cycle of an Apple Tree.* Write one fact about that topic.

_____

Topic: _____

_____

Fact: _____

_____

_____

_____

Children practice various conventions of standard English. Children write routinely for a range of tasks, purposes, and audiences.

Benchmark Vocabulary

Name _____

DIRECTIONS Choose a word from below and draw it in the box. Then write a sentence using the word.

cover   form

_____

_____

Write in Response to Reading

DIRECTIONS Write the heading of your favorite part of the book. Write why you like that part.

_____

_____

_____

_____

_____

Children demonstrate contextual understanding of Benchmark Vocabulary. Children read text closely and use text evidence in their written answers.

Name _____

DIRECTIONS Write a heading from the text.
Draw a picture to show something you learned
from that section.

_____
- -
_____
_____
- -
_____

What I Learned:

 Children analyze and respond to
informational text.

Name _____

DIRECTIONS Circle the nouns that name more than one.

fox   foxes   peach   peaches

wishes   wish   bus   buses

Writing

DIRECTIONS Write one science word from the class picture dictionary. Write what the word means. Draw a picture of the word.

_____

Word: _____

_____

Definition: _____

_____

_____

_____

Children practice various conventions of standard English. Children write routinely for a range of tasks, purposes, and audiences.

Name _____

DIRECTIONS Circle the word for each picture.

f<u>ar</u>m

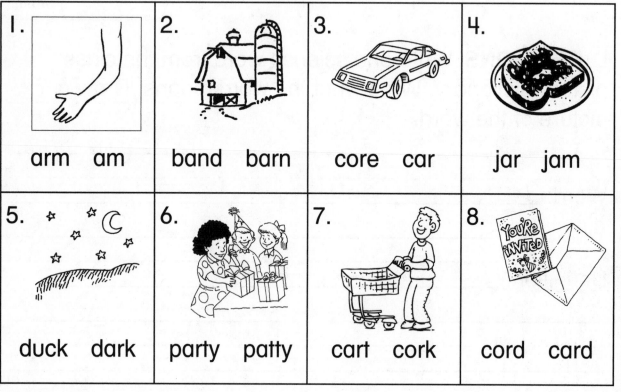

1. arm   am

2. band   barn

3. core   car

4. jar   jam

5. duck   dark

6. party   patty

7. cart   cork

8. cord   card

Find the word that rhymes with .
Circle the letter.

9. **A.** form
    B. far
    C. for

10. **A.** tar
    B. torn
    C. trap

Children apply grade-level phonics and word analysis skills.

Name _____

DIRECTIONS Choose a word from below and draw it in the box. Then write a sentence using the word.

picked   ground   rot

_____

_____

Write in Response to Reading

DIRECTIONS Complete the sentence.

_____

A ripe apple is _____

_____

_____

_____

_____

Children demonstrate contextual understanding of Benchmark Vocabulary. Children read text closely and use text evidence in their written answers.

Name _____

DIRECTIONS Circle the nouns in this sentence.

The seeds in an apple can become a tree.

DIRECTIONS Write a sentence to answer the question.

Where do apple seeds come from?

_____
- -
_____
- -
_____
- -
_____
- -
_____
- -
_____
- -
_____
- -
_____

Children practice various conventions of standard English. Children write routinely for a range of tasks, purposes, and audiences.

Name _____

DIRECTIONS Choose a word from below and draw it in the box. Then write a sentence using the word.

cycle   continues

_____

- -

_____

Write in Response to Reading

DIRECTIONS Circle the word or words to show your opinion. Then complete the sentence.

_____

- - - - - - - - - - - - - - - - - - -

I like / don't like the diagram because _____

_____

- -

_____

- -

_____

- -

_____

Children demonstrate contextual understanding of Benchmark Vocabulary. Children read text closely and use text evidence in their written answers.

Name _____

DIRECTIONS Draw a line to match the noun with the correct verb.

The seed   sprout.

The seeds   sprouts.

DIRECTIONS Draw detailed pictures showing the sequence of steps for how to brush your teeth.

Children practice various conventions of standard English. Children write routinely for a range of tasks, purposes, and audiences.

Name _____

DIRECTIONS Draw the word below in the box. Then write a sentence using the word.

grow

```
┌─────────────────────────────────────────────┐
│                                             │
│                                             │
│                                             │
│                                             │
│                                             │
└─────────────────────────────────────────────┘
```

_____

- -

_____

Write in Response to Reading

DIRECTIONS Write your answer on the lines below.

How are the words *sprout* and *grow* connected?

_____

- -

_____

_____

- -

_____

_____

- -

_____

Children demonstrate contextual understanding of Benchmark Vocabulary. Children read text closely and use text evidence in their written answers.

Name _____

DIRECTIONS Read the words in the box. Write two
sentences that show how some words are connected.

soil	branches	leaves	water
trunk	warmth	sunlight	blossoms

1. words that name parts of an apple tree

_____

_____

_____

_____

2. words that name things an apple tree needs to grow

_____

_____

_____

_____

_____

 Children analyze and respond to
informational text.

Name _____

DIRECTIONS Circle the word that tells that the action happens now.

The seed grows into a plant.

Some apples fall from the trees.

Writing

DIRECTIONS Write the first step for how to brush your teeth.

_____
_____
_____
_____
_____
_____
_____
_____
_____
_____
_____
_____

Children practice various conventions of standard English. Children write routinely for a range of tasks, purposes, and audiences.

Name _____

DIRECTIONS Circle the word for each picture.

h**er**

b**ir**d

s**ur**f

1. short   shirt

2. clerk   click

3. curl   chill

4. barn   burn

5. fern   fan

6. skirt   skit

7. fist   first

8. stir   store

Find the word that has the same vowel sound as .
Circle the letter.

9. **A.** hard
    B. hut
    C. hurt

10. **A.** torn
    B. turn
    C. tune

Children apply grade-level phonics and word analysis skills.

Name _____

DIRECTIONS Choose a word from below and draw it in the box. Then write a sentence using the word.

someday   bottom

Write in Response to Reading

Would you like to plant an oak tree seed?
Write to tell why or why not.

Children demonstrate contextual understanding of Benchmark Vocabulary. Children read text closely and use text evidence in their written answers.

Name _____

DIRECTIONS Circle the words that tell something will happen in the future.

The seed will grow into a bean plant.

The leaves will cover the tree.

DIRECTIONS Recall information from experiences to add a fact to your writing from Lesson 5.

_____
- -
_____
- -
_____
- -
_____
- -
_____
- -
_____
- -
_____
- -

Children practice various conventions of standard English. Children write routinely for a range of tasks, purposes, and audiences.

Name _____

DIRECTIONS Choose a word from below and draw it in the box. Then write a sentence using the word.

sunlight   warmth

Write in Response to Reading

DIRECTIONS Write your answer on the lines below.

What can you find inside apples?

Children demonstrate contextual understanding of Benchmark Vocabulary. Children read text closely and use text evidence in their written answers.

DIRECTIONS Write **is** or **are** to complete the sentences.

A tree _____ a large plant.

The seeds _____ in the apple.

Writing

DIRECTIONS Write a sentence to provide a sense of closure about brushing your teeth.

_____
_____
_____
_____
_____
_____
_____
_____
_____
_____
_____
_____

Children practice various conventions of standard English. Children write routinely for a range of tasks, purposes, and audiences.

Name _____

DIRECTIONS Pick a word from the box that means the same as each pair of words. Write it on the line.

he's	it's	I've	that's	they're
they've	we're	we've	you're	you've

1. I + have	2. we + are
_____	_____
3. it + is	4. that + is
_____	_____
5. you + have	6. they + have
_____	_____
7. we + have	8. he + is
_____	_____
9. they + are	10. you + are
_____	_____

Children apply grade-level phonics and word analysis skills.

Name _____

DIRECTIONS Choose a word below and draw it in the box. Then write a sentence using the word.

sprinkle   carefully   soaks

Write in Response to Reading

Pick a picture from the text. Explain how it shows a key idea in the text.

Children demonstrate contextual understanding of Benchmark Vocabulary. Children read text closely and use text evidence in their written answers.

Name _____

The Best Neighbor Ever

Mrs. Cook is the kindest neighbor ever. Dan's mom got sick, and Mrs. Cook brought dinner. The family's car broke down. Mrs. Cook took Dan to soccer practice. Dan starred in the school play. Mrs. Cook sewed his costume.

One day, Dan said, "How can I help Mrs. Cook? I can't cook or drive or sew."

"You could carry her groceries," Mom said.

"She shops when I'm at school," Dan said.

"You could pick up her newspaper," Mom said.

"She gets it while I'm sleeping," Dan said.

"You could share some of our cake," Mom said.

"She never eats sweets," Dan said.

They looked outside. Mrs. Cook was raking autumn leaves into a big pile. Dan and Mom smiled. Dan put on his jacket. He grabbed a rake and ran next door.

Later, Mrs. Cook looked at the piles of leaves. "You made a bigger pile than I did, Dan. You're the best neighbor ever."

Children read text closely to determine what the text says.

Name _____

Look for Clues
Circle the last sentence in the story. Underline the words at the beginning of the story that connect to the last sentence.

Ask Questions
Why does Mrs. Cook help Dan and his family?

_____

_____

_____

_____

Make Your Case
Circle the name of the person who is the best neighbor in the story.

Make Your Case: Extend Your Ideas
On a sheet of paper, draw a picture of the best neighbor helping. Write words to describe how he or she is helping.

_____

_____

_____

_____

_____

_____

Children read text closely and use text evidence in their written answers.

Name _____

DIRECTIONS Does the verb match the noun?
Circle yes or no.

Trees grow from seeds. Yes/No

A seed grow into a plant. Yes/No

Writing

DIRECTIONS Go back to your writing from Lessons 4, 5, and 6. Add sequence words. Rewrite one step with a time-order word on the lines below.

_____
_____
_____
_____
_____
_____
_____
_____
_____
_____
_____
_____

Children practice various conventions of standard English. Children write routinely for a range of tasks, purposes, and audiences.

Name _____

DIRECTIONS Choose a word from below and draw it in the box. Then write a sentence using the word.

different   loose

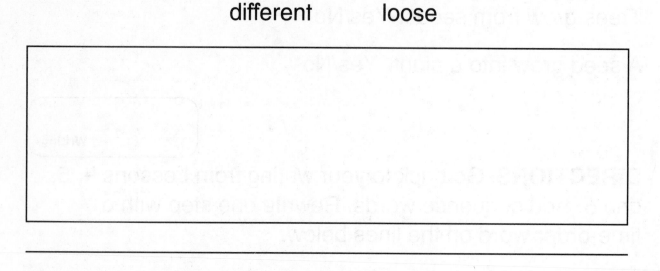

_____

- -

_____

Write in Response to Reading

DIRECTIONS Complete the sentence.

The text tells how a bean seed grows to be a

_____

- -

_____

- -

_____

- -

_____

Children demonstrate contextual understanding of Benchmark Vocabulary. Children read text closely and use text evidence in their written answers.

Name _____

DIRECTIONS Write a complete sentence that tells something about seeds.

_____

_____

_____

_____

DIRECTIONS Write about one revision from your peer review.

_____

_____

_____

_____

_____

_____

_____

_____

 Children practice various conventions of standard English. Children write routinely for a range of tasks, purposes, and audiences.

Name _____

DIRECTIONS Draw the word below in the box. Then write a sentence using the word.

needs

[ ]

_____

_____

Write in Response to Reading

DIRECTIONS Write your answer on the lines. When you plant bean seeds, why should you put them in sunlight?

_____

_____

_____

_____

Copyright © Savvas Learning Company LLC. All Rights Reserved.

Children demonstrate contextual understanding of Benchmark Vocabulary. Children read text vlosely and use text evidence in their written answers.

Name _____

DIRECTIONS Add the correct end mark to the sentence.

An oak tree grows slowly _____

DIRECTIONS Use *How a Seed Grows* and *The Life Cycle of an Apple Tree* to answer the question. Use a complete sentence.

What does a seed need to grow?

_____

_____

_____

_____

_____

_____

_____

Children practice various conventions of standard English. Children write routinely for a range of tasks, purposes, and audiences.

Name _____

DIRECTIONS Circle the word for each picture.

small   small**er**   small**est**

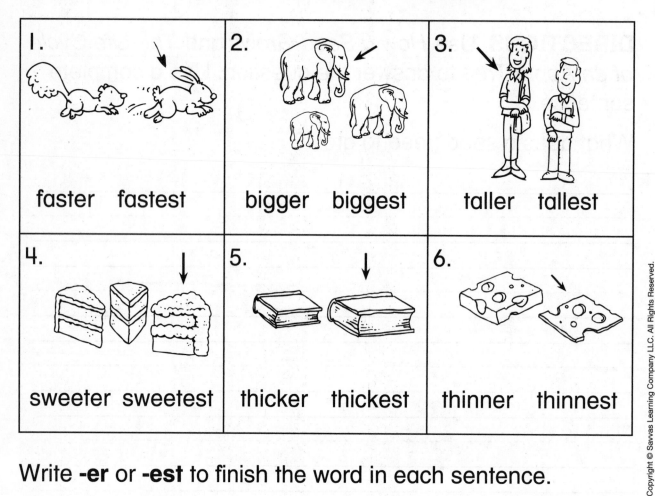

1. faster   fastest

2. bigger   biggest

3. taller   tallest

4. sweeter   sweetest

5. thicker   thickest

6. thinner   thinnest

Write **-er** or **-est** to finish the word in each sentence.

7. The little bird has the few _____ eggs.

8. The little bird has a long _____ tail than the big bird.

Children apply grade-level phonics and word analysis skills.

Name _____

Benchmark Vocabulary

DIRECTIONS Choose a word from below and draw it in the box. Then write a sentence using the word.

conditions   best   worst

_____

- -

_____

Write in Response to Reading

DIRECTIONS Look at the last page of *How a Seed Grows.*

Choose a step from the list. What number is it?
_____

- -

_____

Draw a picture of what happens at this step.

Children demonstrate contextual understanding of Benchmark Vocabulary. Children read text closely and use text evidence in their written answers.

Unit 4 • Module B • Lesson 11 • 293

DIRECTIONS Use the last page of *How a Seed Grows* to answer the questions.

1. What do you put the cress seeds on?

   _____

   _____

   _____

   Circle the text feature where you found the answer.

   paragraph   materials   numbered list

2. What question do you have about the experiment?

   _____

   _____

   _____

   _____

   _____

   _____

   _____

3. Where can you find the answer?

   _____

   _____

   _____

   _____

   _____

   _____

 Children analyze and respond to literary and informational text.

Name _____

DIRECTIONS Write the sentence with the correct end mark.

What kind of seed is this

_____

_____

_____

_____

DIRECTIONS Use the class research to take notes about the life cycle of a frog.

_____

_____

_____

_____

_____

_____

_____

_____

Children practice various conventions of standard English. Children write routinely for a range of tasks, purposes, and audiences.

Name _____

DIRECTIONS Draw the word below in the box. Then write a sentence using the word.

someday

```




```

_____

- -

_____

DIRECTIONS Look at page 20 in *How a Seed Grows.*

Why is a drawing better than a photo to show roots growing?

_____

- -

_____

- -

_____

- -

_____

Children demonstrate contextual understanding of Benchmark Vocabulary. Children read text closely and use text evidence in their written answers.

Name _____

DIRECTIONS Use complete sentences to answer the questions.

What is shown in the diagram in *The Life Cycle of an Apple Tree?*

_____

- -

_____

_____

- -

_____

How are the diagrams in the two texts different?

_____

- -

_____

_____

- -

_____

_____

- -

_____

What do both of these texts have in common?

_____

- -

_____

_____

- -

_____

_____

- -

_____

Children analyze and respond to informational text.

Name _____

DIRECTIONS Write a sentence with the words **in the soil**.

DIRECTIONS Write about the life cycle of a frog.

Children practice various conventions of standard English. Children write routinely for a range of tasks, purposes, and audiences.

Name _____

DIRECTIONS Read each word in the box. Pick a word from the box to finish each sentence. Write it on the line. Read each completed sentence.

fudge	hedge	judge	ledge	smudge

_____

1. Mom made _____ for us to eat.

_____

2. She set it on the _____.

_____

3. Did it fall into the _____?

_____

4. Look, there's a _____ on Bear's face.

_____

5. The _____ thinks Bear ate it too.

Children apply grade-level phonics and word analysis skills.

Name _____

DIRECTIONS Circle the word for each picture.

1. mail   mall

2. tray   tree

3. pal   pail

4. trap   train

5. he   hay

6. pan   pain

Find the word that has the same **long a** sound as [rain picture]. Circle the letter.

7. **A.** clip

   B. clap

   C. clay

8. **A.** man

   B. main

   C. mine

 Children apply grade-level phonics and word analysis skills.

Name _____

DIRECTIONS Choose a word from below and draw it in the box. Then write a sentence using the word.

brave   secret   sparkly

Write in Response to Reading

DIRECTIONS Draw a picture of the moon. Then write words the story uses to tell about the moon.

Children demonstrate contextual understanding of Benchmark Vocabulary. Children read text closely and use text evidence in their written answers.

Name _____

DIRECTIONS Write a short command.

_____

_____

_____

_____

_____

DIRECTIONS Write to tell about King Kafu.

_____

_____

_____

_____

_____

Children practice various conventions of standard English. Children write routinely for a range of tasks, purposes, and audiences.

Name _____

DIRECTIONS Choose a word from below and draw it in the box. Then write a sentence using the word.

bragged   peeping

_____

- -

_____

Write in Response to Reading

DIRECTIONS Write your answer on the lines.

What is King Kafu's secret?

_____
- -
_____
- -
_____
- -
_____
- -
_____

Children demonstrate contextual understanding of Benchmark Vocabulary. Children read text closely and use text evidence in their written answers.

Name _____

DIRECTIONS Add an end mark to each sentence.

Look out

Please turn on the light

DIRECTIONS Think about the beginning of *King Kafu and the Moon*. Write to tell what happens.

_____

_____

_____

_____

_____

_____

_____

_____

_____

_____

Children practice various conventions of standard English. Children write routinely for a range of tasks, purposes, and audiences.

Name _____

DIRECTIONS Write each underlined word correctly.
Add the ' where it belongs.

1. <u>Janes</u> drum = _____ drum

2. <u>dogs</u> bone = _____ bone

3. <u>Moms</u> cup = _____ cup

4. <u>babys</u> crib = _____ crib

5. <u>pets</u> beds = _____ beds

Pick a word from the box to match each picture.
Write it on the line.

girls'	Matt's

6. _____ lunch

7. _____ games

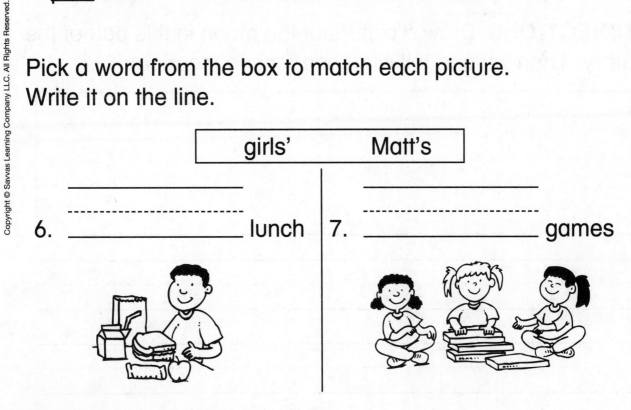

Children apply grade-level phonics and word
analysis skills.

Name _____

DIRECTIONS Choose a word from below and draw it in the box. Then write a sentence using the word.

piece   disappearing   capture

```
┌─────────────────────────────────────────┐
│                                         │
│                                         │
│                                         │
│                                         │
│                                         │
└─────────────────────────────────────────┘
```

_____

- -

_____

Write in Response to Reading

DIRECTIONS Draw a picture of the moon in this part of the story. Then write to tell what happens to the moon.

```
┌─────────────────────────────────────────┐
│                                         │
│                                         │
│                                         │
│                                         │
│                                         │
└─────────────────────────────────────────┘
```

_____

- -

_____

- -

Children demonstrate contextual understanding of Benchmark Vocabulary. Children read text closely and use text evidence in their written answers.

Name _____

Look Out for Wildlife

Wild animals are amazing! They can be scary too! Mom and Dad took me to Yellowstone National Park. Many wild animals live in its fields and woods.

One day we drove through the park. We saw a herd of bison. Another name for bison is buffalo. A bison has shaggy hair and a big bump on its back. We drove on and reached a dead end. Suddenly a huge bear came toward the car. It looked mad!

Dad said, "Don't worry. She can't get in the car." Dad slowly backed up the car. Then we drove away. The huge bear watched us go. My heart was beating fast. But I still took some pictures. They show the mother bear—and its cub! Dad said the bear was just protecting its baby.

Children read text closely to determine what the text says.

Name _____

Look for Clues
Circle the name of an animal. Underline a detail that tells about the animal. Circle the name of another animal. Underline a detail about the animal.

Ask Questions
Write one thing you would like to know about Yellowstone National Park.

_____

_____

_____

Make Your Case
Finish the sentence: Dad backed up to go away from

_____

_____

Make Your Case: Extend Your Ideas
What was the bear doing? Draw a box around the answer in the story. What might the bear have done if Dad had not backed up?

_____

_____

_____

_____

Children read text closely to determine what the text says.

Name _____

DIRECTIONS Write a statement. Then write a question.

_____
- -
_____
- -
_____
- -
_____
- -
_____

Writing

DIRECTIONS Think about what happens next in the story. Write to tell what happens. Use time-order words.

_____
- -
_____
- -
_____
- -
_____
- -
_____

Children practice various conventions of standard English. Children write routinely for a range of tasks, purposes, and audiences.

Name _____

DIRECTIONS Choose a word from below and draw it in the box. Then write a sentence using the word.

announcement   confused   reward

[empty box]

_____

- -

_____

_____

- -

_____

Write in Response to Reading

DIRECTIONS Write your answer on the lines.
What does King Kafu ask the villagers to do?

_____

- -

_____

- -

_____

- -

_____

 Children demonstrate contextual understanding of Benchmark Vocabulary. Children read text closely and use text evidence in their written answers.

Name _____

DIRECTIONS Write an exclamation.

_____

_____

_____

_____

_____

_____

Writing

DIRECTIONS Write a plan for your story.

_____

Characters _____

_____

_____

Setting _____

_____

Events _____

_____

_____

_____

_____

Children practice various conventions of standard English. Children write routinely for a range of tasks, purposes, and audiences.

Name _____

DIRECTIONS Choose a word from below and draw it in the box. Then write a sentence using the word.

searched   hiding

Write in Response to Reading

DIRECTIONS Write your answer on the lines below.

What do the villagers use to help them catch the moon?

Children demonstrate contextual understanding of Benchmark Vocabulary. Children read text closely and use text evidence in their written answers.

Name _____

DIRECTIONS Circle the noun that should end with **'s**.

The boy searched the king castle.

The boy idea was to fill the streets with lights.

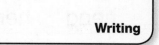

DIRECTIONS Think of three events for your story.
Write your plan.

_____

Event 1 _____

_____

_____

Event 2 _____

_____

_____

Event 3 _____

_____

_____

Children practice various conventions of
standard English. Children write routinely for a
range of tasks, purposes, and audiences.

Name _____

DIRECTIONS Circle the word for each picture.

1.	2.	3.
head herd	sail seal	berry bread
4.	5.	6.
leaf loaf	jeans jar	clean clang

Circle the words that finish each sentence.

7. **Please / Place** pass the **peas / bees**.

8. I hit my **head / help** when I fell.

9. I **read / rang** my book at the **beach / birch**.

 Children apply grade-level phonics and word analysis skills.

Name _____

DIRECTIONS Choose a word from below and draw it in the box. Then write a sentence using the word.

dizzy   festival

```



```
_____

- -

_____

Write in Response to Reading

DIRECTIONS Write your answer on the lines.

What do the villagers learn about the moon?

_____

- -

_____

- -

_____

- -

_____

Children demonstrate contextual understanding of Benchmark Vocabulary. Children read text closely and use text evidence in their written answers.

Name _____

DIRECTIONS Circle the noun that should end with '.

The kids backpacks are in the classroom.

The teacher put the girls coats on the hooks.

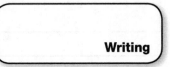

Writing

DIRECTIONS Think of a conclusion for your story.
Write your plan.

_____
- -
_____
_____
- -
_____
_____
- -
_____
_____
- -
_____
_____
- -
_____

 Children practice various conventions of standard English. Children write routinely for a range of tasks, purposes, and audiences.

Name _____

DIRECTIONS Choose a word from below and draw it in the box. Then write a sentence using the word.

afraid   bright

_____

- -

_____

Write in Response to Reading

DIRECTIONS Write a sentence to tell about the ending of *King Kafu and the Moon.*

_____

- -

_____

- -

_____

_____

- -

_____

Children demonstrate contextual understanding of Benchmark Vocabulary. Children read text closely and use text evidence in their written answers.

DIRECTIONS Choose two words or phrases from the story. Write each word or phrase. Then write a sentence with the word or phrase.

Word/Phrase 1: _____

_____

_____

_____

_____

Word/Phrase 2: _____

_____

_____

_____

_____

 Children analyze and respond to literary texts.

Name _____

DIRECTIONS Write the sentence. Add ' or **'s** to the underlined noun.

The <u>moon</u> light is bright.

_____

- - - - - - - - - - - - - - - - - - - -

_____

- - - - - - - - - - - - - - - - - - - -

_____

DIRECTIONS Think of sensory words you can add to your story. Write the words.

_____

- - - - - - - - - - - - - - - - - - - -

_____

- - - - - - - - - - - - - - - - - - - -

_____

- - - - - - - - - - - - - - - - - - - -

_____

- - - - - - - - - - - - - - - - - - - -

_____

Children practice various conventions of standard English. Children write routinely for a range of tasks, purposes, and audiences.

Name _____

DIRECTIONS Add **-ed** to each word.
Write the new word on the line.

fr**ied**

1. dry _____

2. copy _____

3. spy _____

4. try _____

Add **-er** and **-est** to each word.
Write the new words on the lines.

	Add -er	Add -est
5. silly		
6. funny		
7. happy		
8. easy		

Children apply grade-level phonics and word analysis skills.

Name _____

DIRECTIONS Draw a picture of the word below in the box. Then write a sentence using the word.

glows

_____
- -
_____

Write in Response to Reading

DIRECTIONS Complete the sentence to tell a detail about the moon.

_____
- -
The moon _____
- -
_____
- -
_____
- -
_____

Children demonstrate contextual understanding of Benchmark Vocabulary. Children read text closely and use text evidence in their written answers.

Name _____

DIRECTIONS Write a question you have about the text.
Then write the answer to your question.

_____

Question: _____

_____

_____

_____

_____

_____

_____

_____

Answer: _____

_____

_____

_____

_____

_____

_____

Children analyze and respond to informational texts.

Name _____

DIRECTIONS Rewrite the sentence. Add a detail.

The sun is a star.

_____

_____

_____

_____

Writing

DIRECTIONS Write a plan for your story.

_____

Characters _____

_____

Setting _____

_____

Events _____

_____

_____

_____

Children practice various conventions of standard English. Children write routinely for a range of tasks, purposes, and audiences.

Name _____

DIRECTIONS Choose a word from below and draw it in the box. Then write a sentence using the word.

closer   valleys

Write in Response to Reading

DIRECTIONS Write your answer on the lines.

What is one way the moon is like Earth?

_____

_____

_____

_____

_____

Children demonstrate contextual understanding of Benchmark Vocabulary. Children read text closely and use text evidence in their written answers.

Name _____

DIRECTIONS Add letters to spell words.

_____at   _____at   _____a_____e   _____a_____e

DIRECTIONS Think of two events for your story.
Write your plan.

_____

Event 1 _____

_____

_____

_____

Event 2 _____

_____

_____

_____

Children practice various conventions of
standard English. Children write routinely for a
range of tasks, purposes, and audiences.

Name _____

DIRECTIONS Choose a word from below and draw it in the box. Then write a sentence using the word.

smaller   possible   orbit

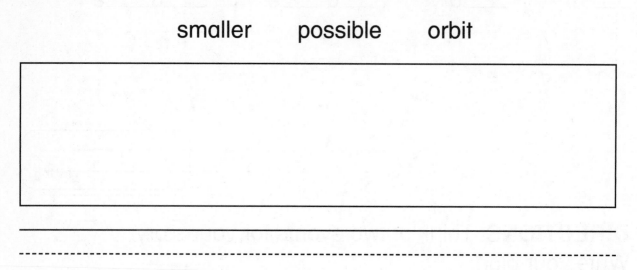

_____

- -

_____

Write in Response to Reading

DIRECTIONS Write your answer on the lines.

What is one interesting fact you learned about the sun, the moon, or Earth?

_____

- -

_____

_____

- -

_____

_____

- -

_____

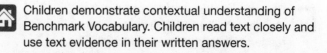 Children demonstrate contextual understanding of Benchmark Vocabulary. Children read text closely and use text evidence in their written answers.

Name _____

DIRECTIONS Write the words. Add **er.** Then write a sentence that uses one of the words.

_____   _____

slow _____   fast _____

_____

_____

_____

_____

Writing

DIRECTIONS Think of a conclusion for your story. Write your plan.

_____

_____

_____

_____

Children practice various conventions of standard English. Children write routinely for a range of tasks, purposes, and audiences.

Name _____

DIRECTIONS Circle the word for each picture.

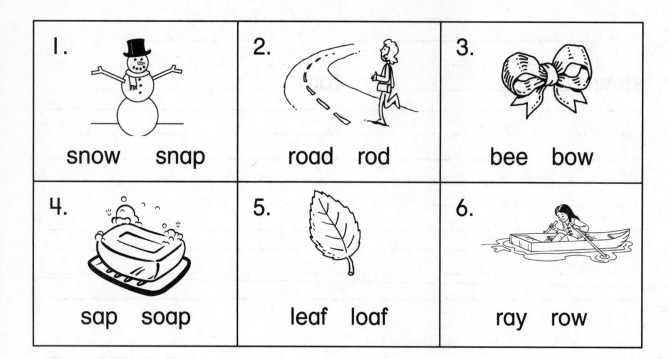

I.	2.	3.
snow snap	road rod	bee bow
4.	5.	6.
sap soap	leaf loaf	ray row

Write the letters that finish the words in each sentence.

7. The g_____t drank from the b_____l.

8. They looked high and l_____, but they could not

   find the r_____d.

Children apply grade-level phonics and word analysis skills.

Name _____

DIRECTIONS Choose a word from below and draw it in the box. Then write a sentence using the word.

crescent   astronauts

_____
_____
_____

Write in Response to Reading

DIRECTIONS Write your answer on the lines.
Why can we see the moon?

_____
_____
_____
_____
_____
_____

Children demonstrate contextual understanding of Benchmark Vocabulary. Children read text closely and use text evidence in their written answers.

Name _____

DIRECTIONS Write the date correctly.
october 31 2015

_____
- -
_____
- -
_____

Writing

DIRECTIONS Write details about the moon that you can add to your story.

_____
- -
_____
_____
- -
_____
_____
- -
_____
_____
- -
_____

Children practice various conventions of standard English. Children write routinely for a range of tasks, purposes, and audiences.

Name _____

DIRECTIONS Choose a word from below and draw it in the box. Then write a sentence using the word.

disappearing   crescent

Write in Response to Reading

DIRECTIONS Draw one way the moon can look. Then write a sentence that tells how it looks.

Children demonstrate contextual understanding of Benchmark Vocabulary. Children read text closely and use text evidence in their written answers.

Name _____

DIRECTIONS Write your answers on the lines.
First, look at page 25 of *Let's Visit the Moon*.
What does the text say? We see the moon because

_____

- -

_____

Now look at pages 26 and 27. Why do we only see part of
the moon sometimes?

_____

- -

_____

_____

- -

_____

_____

- -

_____

Next, look at pages 8 and 9 of *King Kafu and the Moon*.
What does King Kafu say? King Kafu says the moon is

_____

- -

_____

What is actually happening to the moon?

_____

- -

_____

_____

- -

Children analyze and respond to literary and
informational texts.

Name _____

DIRECTIONS Add **to, too,** or **two** to the sentence.

I would like to go _____ the moon.

Writing

DIRECTIONS Look over your story. Check off what you have done. Write any new ideas you have.

☐ The sentences in my story tell about visiting the moon.

☐ Each sentence begins with a capital letter.

☐ Each sentence ends with an end mark.

☐ I have checked the spelling of words I wasn't sure of.

_____

_____
_____

_____
_____

_____

Children practice various conventions of standard English. Children write routinely for a range of tasks, purposes, and audiences.

Name _____

DIRECTIONS Circle the word for each picture.

1.	stub scrub	2.	sting string
3.	those three	4.	spring sing
5.	squeeze sneeze	6.	stripe ripe

Write the letters that finish the words in each sentence.

7. She _____ew the ball _____ough

   the _____een door.

8. I had a sore _____oat.

 Children apply grade-level phonics and word analysis skills.

Name _____

DIRECTIONS Choose a word from below and draw it in the box. Then write a sentence using the word.

hiding   glows

Write in Response to Reading

DIRECTIONS Circle the text you like better.
Tell why you like it.

I like *King Kafu and the Moon / Let's Visit the Moon* better
because

_____

_____

_____

_____

_____

Children demonstrate contextual understanding of
Benchmark Vocabulary. Children read text closely
and use text evidence in their written answers.

Is Your Polar Bear Happy?

What would you do with an unhappy elephant? Some scientists study animal behavior. They can answer this question.

Some scientists watch animals in the wild. Others see how people's pets act. Still others watch zoo animals. They see how the animals behave. Is the animal comfortable in its zoo home? Does it eat enough? How does it get along with other animals?

At one zoo, a polar bear seemed upset. He swam up and down his pool all day. Scientists watched the bear for several days. They took notes. They decided to give the bear more toys. They played games with him.

At another zoo, some elephants were causing problems. Scientists watched their behavior. Then they gave the elephants more exercise. They fed them different foods. They put the foods in feeders off the ground. The elephants behaved better.

People don't understand everything about animals. These scientists help us learn more.

 Children read text closely to determine what the text says.

Name _____

Look for Clues

Underline sentences that tell about animal behaviors that scientists study.

Ask Questions

What question would you ask a scientist about how animals behave?

_____

- -

_____

Make Your Case

Box words that show what happens when a scientist helps an unhappy animal.

Make Your Case: Extend Your Ideas

Draw the elephants that were causing problems. Then draw them after the scientists helped them. Write what happened.

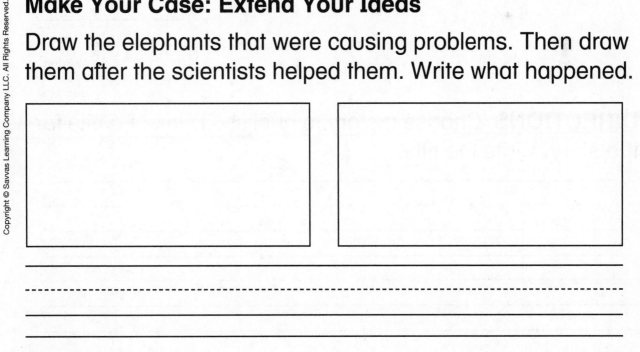

_____

- -

_____

- -

_____

Children read text closely to determine what the text says.

Name _____

DIRECTIONS Add an adjective to the sentence. Then write your own sentence using one or more adjectives.

_____

We saw the _____ moon in the sky.

_____

_____

_____

_____

DIRECTIONS Choose a story to publish. Think of a title for the story. Write the title.

_____

_____

_____

_____

Children practice various conventions of standard English. Children write routinely for a range of tasks, purposes, and audiences.

Name _____

DIRECTIONS Circle the word for each picture.

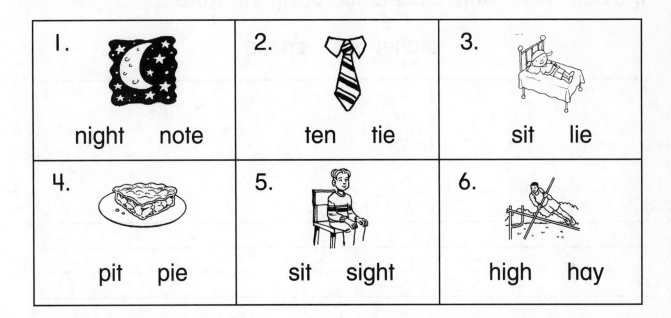

1. night note	2. ten tie	3. sit lie
4. pit pie	5. sit sight	6. high hay

Read the sentences.
Circle the words with the **long i** sound spelled **ie** and **igh**.
Underline the words with the **long e** sound spelled **ie**.

7. I would like another piece of bread.

8. He believes that he is right.

9. I am sorry that I lied to you.

10. The sight of the green field makes us happy.

Children apply grade-level phonics and word
analysis skills.

Lesson 1

Name _____

DIRECTIONS Choose a word from below and draw it in the box. Then write a sentence using the word.

planet   space

DIRECTIONS Write your answer on the lines.

What can orbit the sun?

Children demonstrate contextual understanding of Benchmark Vocabulary. Children read text closely and use text evidence in their written answers.

Name _____

DIRECTIONS Write 3 words that end with **-un**.

_____

_____

_____

DIRECTIONS Write 1 or 2 factual sentences about the night sky.

_____

_____

_____

_____

_____

_____

_____

Children practice various conventions of standard English. Children write routinely for a range of tasks, purposes, and audiences.

Name _____

DIRECTIONS Draw the word below in the box. Then write a sentence using the word.

hotter

Do you like to read about the sun? Tell why or why not.

Children demonstrate contextual understanding of Benchmark Vocabulary. Children read text closely and use text evidence in their written answers.

Name _____

DIRECTIONS Write 3 words that end with **-it.**

_____

_____

_____

Writing

DIRECTIONS Draw and label a picture to describe what you have observed about the sun.

_____

_____

_____

Children practice various conventions of standard English. Children write routinely for a range of tasks, purposes, and audiences.

Name _____

DIRECTIONS Circle the word for each picture.

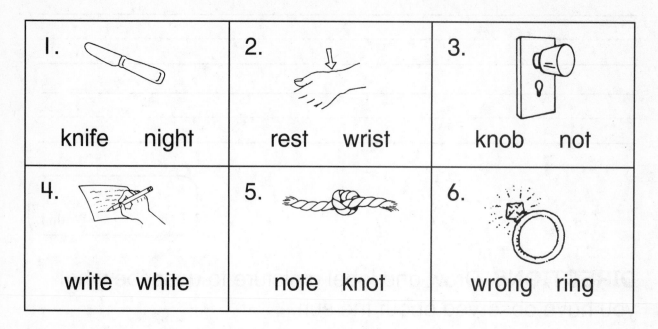

1. knife   night

2. rest   wrist

3. knob   not

4. write   white

5. note   knot

6. wrong   ring

Find the word that has the same beginning sound
as the picture.
Circle the letter.

7. **A.** wren

   B. when

   C. went

8. **A.** sneak

   B. kite

   C. knock

Children apply grade-level phonics and word analysis
skills.

Name _____

DIRECTIONS Draw the word below in the box. Then write a sentence using the word.

dwarf

```
┌─────────────────────────────────────────┐
│                                         │
│                                         │
│                                         │
│                                         │
│                                         │
│                                         │
└─────────────────────────────────────────┘
```

_____

- -

_____

Write in Response to Reading

DIRECTIONS Write your answer on the lines below.

How can a picture or diagram help you understand the solar system?

_____

- -

_____

_____

- -

_____

_____

- -

_____

Children demonstrate contextual understanding of Benchmark Vocabulary. Children read text closely and use text evidence in their written answers.

DIRECTIONS Circle the word to complete the sentence.

The (suns / sun's) heat warms Earth.

Writing

DIRECTIONS Draw a simple diagram of the sun and planets. Label the parts.

Children practice various conventions of standard English. Children write routinely for a range of tasks, purposes, and audiences.

Name _____

DIRECTIONS What did you learn about the giant planets? Draw a picture to show what you know. Write a sentence to tell about your picture.

Children analyze and respond to literary and informational text.

Name _____

DIRECTIONS Circle the word that needs a capital letter.

light   sky   saturn

Writing

DIRECTIONS Write an introduction for your planet book.

_____
- -
_____
_____
- -
_____
_____
- -
_____
_____
- -
_____
_____
- -
_____
_____
- -
_____
_____
- -
_____

Children practice various conventions of standard English. Children write routinely for a range of tasks, purposes, and audiences.

Name _____

DIRECTIONS Pick a word from the box to finish
each compound word.
Write it on the line. Draw a line to the picture it matches.

| boat | man | paper | watch |

1. news_____

2. row_____

3. wrist_____

4. snow_____

Find the compound word. Circle the letter.

5. **A.** raining   6. **A.** popcorn   7. **A.** mitten

   B. rainy   **B.** puppy   **B.** marching

   C. raincoat   **C.** popping   **C.** backpack

Children apply grade-level phonics and word
analysis skills.

Name _____

DIRECTIONS Choose a word from below and draw it in the box. Then write a sentence using the word.

closest   strongest

_____

- -

_____

Write in Response to Reading

Would you like to walk on the moon? Tell why or why not.

_____

- -

_____

- -

_____

- -

_____

- -

_____

Children demonstrate contextual understanding of Benchmark Vocabulary. Children read text closely and use text evidence in their written answers.

Conventions

Name _____

DIRECTIONS Circle the word that is spelled incorrectly. Write the word correctly on the line.

_____

Do yu see the sun? _____

Writing

DIRECTIONS Write 3 questions that you will answer in your planet book.

_____
_____
_____
_____
_____
_____
_____
_____
_____
_____
_____
_____
_____
_____

Children practice various conventions of standard English. Children write routinely for a range of tasks, purposes, and audiences.

Name _____

DIRECTIONS Choose a word from below and draw it in the box. Then write a sentence using the word.

tools   study

Write in Response to Reading

DIRECTIONS Write your answer on the lines.

What does a rover look like?

_____

_____

_____

_____

_____

_____

_____

Children demonstrate contextual understanding of Benchmark Vocabulary. Children read text closely and use text evidence in their written answers.

Name _____

DIRECTIONS Circle the word that is spelled incorrectly. Write the word.

_____

Mars is wun of the planets. _____

_____

_____

Writing

DIRECTIONS Write the answer to one of your questions that you can include in your planet book.

_____

_____

_____

_____

_____

_____

_____

_____

_____

_____

_____

Children practice various conventions of standard English. Children write routinely for a range of tasks, purposes, and audiences.

Name _____

DIRECTIONS Circle the word for each picture.

1. blew black	2. glue glow	3. joke juice
4. sit suit	5. news nose	6. flow flew

Read the words in the box.
Pick a word to finish each sentence.

bruise	drew	true

7. It is _____ that I like grapes.

8. He has a _____ on his leg.

9. My sister _____ this picture.

 Children apply grade-level phonics and word analysis skills.

Name _____

DIRECTIONS Choose a word from below and draw it in the box. Then write a sentence using the word.

brightly   larger

```




```

_____

What is the most interesting fact you learned about the sun?

_____

_____

_____

_____

Children demonstrate contextual understanding of Benchmark Vocabulary. Children read text closely and use text evidence in their written answers.

Name _____

Finding a Voice

Cam was unhappy. He would be in the hospital for many weeks. He had a tube in his throat. He could not talk. How could he tell his mom or dad that he wanted something? How could he talk with friends?

One day a nurse had an idea. She found a special tool for him to use. Cam's eyes lit up when she gave it to him. The tool looked like a computer keyboard with a screen. Cam typed a word. He typed a sentence. Then he pushed a button. The computer said what Cam typed!

This computer uses special software. It helps people who have difficulty speaking. It gives them a "voice." The software can fit on the tiniest computers. This software has given people freedom to communicate. That's something to shout about!

 Children read text closely to determine what the text says.

Name _____

Look for Clues

Circle the sentence that tells how Cam felt **before** he got his computer. Underline clues that show how Cam felt **after** he got the computer.

Look for Clues: Extend Your Ideas

Think about how Cam felt before he got the computer. Box the sentences that tell why Cam felt this way.

Ask Questions

What do you wonder about the special software? Write two questions.

_____
_____
_____
_____
_____
_____
_____
_____

Ask Questions: Extend Your Ideas

Suppose you wonder how the special software helps people. Underline the sentences in the text that will answer that question.

Make Your Case

What do you think is the most interesting fact about the software? Box the fact in the text.

Children read text closely to determine what the text says.

DIRECTIONS Add letters to spell words.

_____ed   _____ed   _____ed

Writing

DIRECTIONS Write a detail about your planet that you can put in your planet book.

_____

- -

_____

- -

_____

- -

_____

- -

_____

- -

_____

Children practice various conventions of standard English. Children write routinely for a range of tasks, purposes, and audiences.

Name _____

DIRECTIONS Choose a word from below and draw it in the box. Then write a sentence using the word.

center   seasons

```



```
_____
- -
_____
- -
_____

Write in Response to Reading

What is the most interesting thing you learned from the section called "Planets and the Sun"?

_____
- -
_____
- -
_____
- -
_____

Children demonstrate contextual understanding of Benchmark Vocabulary. Children read text closely and use text evidence in their written answers.

Name _____

DIRECTIONS Circle the correct word to complete the sentence.

The sun (seems / seem) to move across the sky.

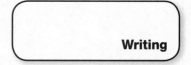

Writing

DIRECTIONS Create a text feature to include in your planet book.

 Children practice various conventions of standard English. Children write routinely for a range of tasks, purposes, and audiences.

Name _____

DIRECTIONS Choose a word from below and draw it in the box. Then write a sentence using the word.

spins   rises   sets

```

┌─────────────────────────────────────────┐
│                                         │
│                                         │
│                                         │
│                                         │
│                                         │
│                                         │
└─────────────────────────────────────────┘
```

_____

_____

_____

_____

Write in Response to Reading

Write one thing you learned from the book.

_____

_____

_____

_____

_____

_____

_____

Children demonstrate contextual understanding of Benchmark Vocabulary. Children read text closely and use text evidence in their written answers.

Name _____

DIRECTIONS Circle the correct word to complete the sentence.

Tomorrow we will (wrote / write) about the planet.

DIRECTIONS Write a conclusion to your planet book.

_____

_____

_____

_____

_____

_____

_____

_____

_____

_____

_____

_____

_____

Children practice various conventions of standard English. Children write routinely for a range of tasks, purposes, and audiences.

Name _____

DIRECTIONS Add **-ly** or **-ful** to the word in ( ).
Write the new word on the line.

(play)

_____

1. The dog is _____ .

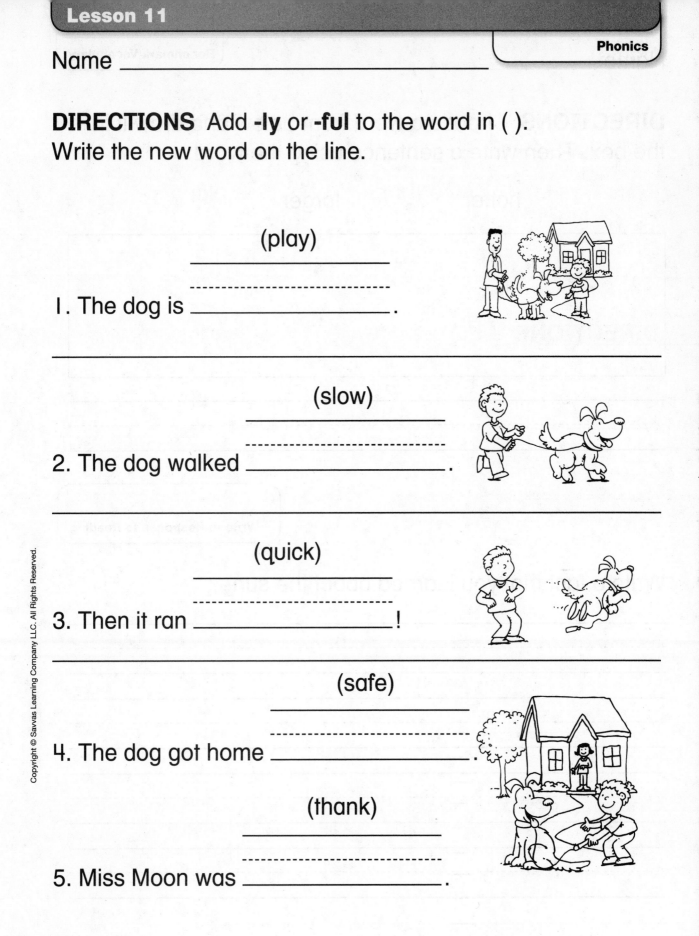

(slow)

_____

2. The dog walked _____ .

(quick)

_____

3. Then it ran _____ !

(safe)

_____

4. The dog got home _____ .

(thank)

_____

5. Miss Moon was _____ .

Children apply grade-level phonics and word
analysis skills.

Name _____

DIRECTIONS Choose a word from below and draw it in the box. Then write a sentence using the word.

hotter   larger

[drawing box]

_____
- -
_____

Write in Response to Reading

Write a fact that you learned about the sun.

_____
- -
_____
- -
_____
- -
_____
- -
_____

Children demonstrate contextual understanding of Benchmark Vocabulary. Children read text closely and use text evidence in their written answers.

Name _____

DIRECTIONS Write one way the two texts are the same.

_____
- -
_____
- -
_____
- -
_____
- -
_____

Write one way the two texts are different.

_____
- -
_____
- -
_____
- -
_____
- -
_____

Children analyze and respond to literary and informational text.

DIRECTIONS Find the mistakes in the sentence. Write the sentence correctly.

earth and venus ar planet

_____

_____

_____

_____

_____

Writing

DIRECTIONS Rewrite one sentence from your planet book with correct capitalization, spelling, and punctuation.

_____

_____

_____

_____

_____

_____

_____

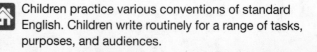

Children practice various conventions of standard English. Children write routinely for a range of tasks, purposes, and audiences.

Name _____

DIRECTIONS Choose a word from below and draw it in the box. Then write a sentence using the word.

dwarf   center

Write in Response to Reading

What questions do you have after reading about the sun and the planets?

Children demonstrate contextual understanding of Benchmark Vocabulary. Children read text closely and use text evidence in their written answers.

Name _____

DIRECTIONS Choose two of the eight big planets.
Draw the two planets.

Write the names of the planets under the drawings.

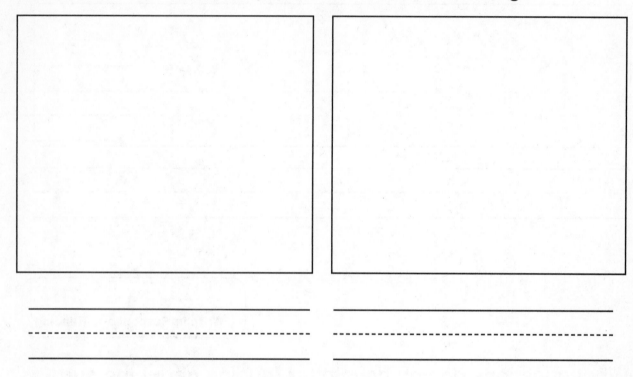

_____   _____

- -

Tell how the two planets are the same.
Tell how they are different.

_____

- -

_____

_____

- -

_____

_____

- -

_____

 Children analyze and respond to literary and
informational text.

Name _____

DIRECTIONS Find the mistakes in the sentence.
Write the sentence correctly.

do you think it's fun to read about the planets

_____

_____

_____

Writing

What do you still need to fix? Write your notes here.

_____

_____

_____

_____

_____

_____

Children practice various conventions of
standard English. Children write routinely for a
range of tasks, purposes, and audiences.

Name _____

DIRECTIONS Circle the word for each picture.

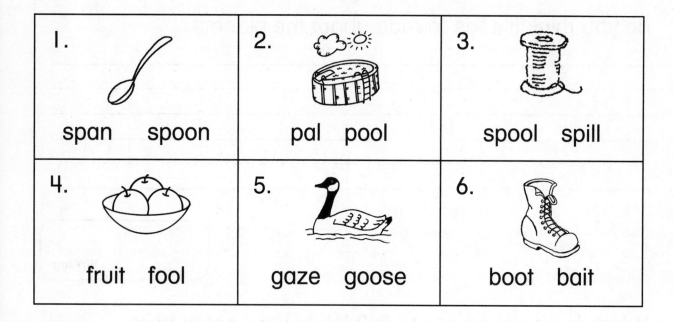

1.	2.	3.
span spoon	pal pool	spool spill
4.	5.	6.
fruit fool	gaze goose	boot bait

Pick a word to finish each sentence.
Write the word in the sentence.

7. The _____ blocked the cars on the road.

    moose   mouse

8. I need a _____ to clean this mess!

    boot   broom

 Children apply grade-level phonics and word analysis skills.

Name _____

DIRECTIONS Pick a word from the box to match each picture. Write it on the line.

| cloud | clown | flower | house |

1.

_____

- -

_____

2.

_____

- -

3.

_____

- -

_____

4.

_____

- -

Unscramble the letters to make a word.

_____

- - - - - - - - - - - - - - - - - - - -

uold   _____

wtno   _____

- -

Pick a word to finish each sentence. Write it on the line.

_____

- - - - - - - - - - - - - - - - -

5. The radio was too _____.

_____

- - - - - - - - - - - - - - - - -

6. I like to shop in _____.

Children apply grade-level phonics and word analysis skills.

Benchmark Vocabulary

DIRECTIONS Choose a word from below and draw it in the box. Then write a sentence using the word.

neighborhoods   study   traditional

Write in Response to Reading

DIRECTIONS Complete the sentence.

The United States is _____

Children demonstrate contextual understanding of Benchmark Vocabulary. Children read text closely and use text evidence in their written answers.

Name _____

DIRECTIONS Combine the two sentences to form a compound sentence.

We played basketball. We had fun.

_____
_____
_____
_____

Writing

DIRECTIONS Write about the country from the book you would like to visit.

_____
_____
_____
_____
_____
_____
_____
_____

Children practice various conventions of standard English. Children write routinely for a range of tasks, purposes, and audiences.

Name _____

DIRECTIONS Choose a word from below and draw it in the box. Then write a sentence using the word.

peek   prepare   designs

Write in Response to Reading

DIRECTIONS Write one sentence that tells a fact about Ama.

Children demonstrate contextual understanding of Benchmark Vocabulary. Children read text closely and use text evidence in their written answers.

Name _____

DIRECTIONS Add details to the sentence. Write the new sentence on the lines.

We eat dinner.

_____
- -
_____
_____
- -
_____
- -
_____

Writing

DIRECTIONS Add reasons to support your opinion.

_____
- -
_____
_____
- -
_____
_____
- -
_____

Children practice various conventions of standard English. Children write routinely for a range of tasks, purposes, and audiences.

Name _____

DIRECTIONS Circle the word for each picture.

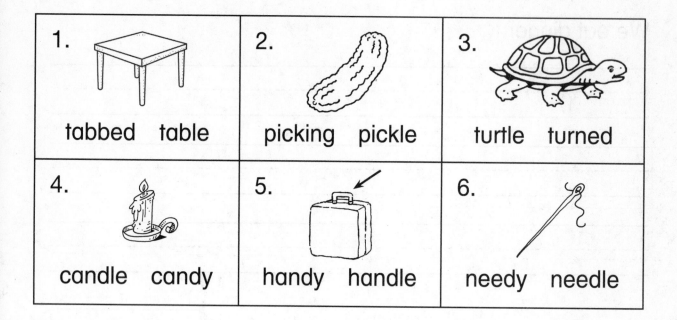

1.	2.	3.
tabbed table	picking pickle	turtle turned
4.	5.	6.
candle candy	handy handle	needy needle

Find the word that has the same ending sound as ![bottle]. Circle the letter.

7. **A.** litter

    B. lightly

    C. little

8. **A.** purple

    B. purred

    C. purest

 Children apply grade-level phonics and word analysis skills.

Name _____

DIRECTIONS Choose a word from below and draw it in the box. Then write a sentence using the word.

tasty   celebrates   lively

Write in Response to Reading

What does Raul enjoy about his family?

_____

- -

_____

- -

_____

What does Britta enjoy doing?

_____

- -

_____

- -

_____

Children demonstrate contextual understanding of Benchmark Vocabulary. Children read text closely and use text evidence in their written answers.

Name _____

A Horse Named Chester

Did you ever see a horse in a store? Chester goes into stores. Chester is special. He is a service horse. Chester's owner, Mike, cannot see. Chester helps Mike every day. Chester leads him along. He helps Mike cross streets. Chester helps Mike find his way.

Chester looks much like other horses. But he is much smaller. He is the size of a large dog.

People have used service dogs for many years. Some people think horses are better helpers. Small horses like Chester are gentle. They are friendly. They can learn to help people. They can live for 30 years or more.

Trainers teach service horses to do their jobs. Service horses are good helpers. They are also great friends.

 Children read text closely to determine what the text says.

Name _____

Look for Clues
Circle the sentence that tells what the writer thinks about service horses.

Ask Questions
Write one question about service horses.

_____

- -

_____

- -

_____

- -

_____

- -

_____

Ask Questions: Extend Your Ideas
Underline the sentences in the story that relate to your question.

Make Your Case
Underline the words in the text that tell what you learned about service horses.

Make Your Case: Extend Your Ideas
Write what you learned about service horses.

_____

- -

_____

- -

_____

- -

_____

Children read text closely to determine what
the text says.

Name _____

DIRECTIONS Write the date that you were born. Be sure to include commas.

_____

_____

_____

DIRECTIONS Add a sense of closure to your opinion writing from Lessons 1 and 2.

_____

_____

_____

_____

_____

_____

Children practice various conventions of standard English. Children write routinely for a range of tasks, purposes, and audiences.

Name _____

DIRECTIONS Choose a word from below and draw it in the box. Then write a sentence using the word.

serves   several   blurs

Write in Response to Reading

DIRECTIONS Write your response in complete sentences.

Name 3 things the text mentions about Kenyans.

Children demonstrate contextual understanding of Benchmark Vocabulary. Children read text closely and use text evidence in their written answers.

Name _____

DIRECTIONS Write your name with **'s** and something that belongs to you.

_____

- -

_____

- -

_____

- -

_____

Writing

DIRECTIONS Write a complete sentence telling your favorite custom in your family.

_____

- -

_____

- -

_____

- -

_____

 Children practice various conventions of standard English. Children write routinely for a range of tasks, purposes, and audiences.

Name _____

DIRECTIONS Choose a word from below and draw it in the box. Then write a sentence using the word.

respect   sip   rude

- -

DIRECTIONS Write your answer on the lines. Use a complete sentence.

Why is Suhe still learning to speak English?

_____
- -
_____
- -
_____
- -
_____

Children demonstrate contextual understanding of Benchmark Vocabulary. Children read text closely and use text evidence in their written answers.

Name _____

DIRECTIONS Circle the correct word to complete the sentence.

That is (a / an) good poem.

That is (a / an) excellent poem.

Writing

DIRECTIONS Write one or more reasons to support your opinion from Lesson 4.

_____

- -

_____

- -

_____

- -

_____

- -

_____

- -

_____

- -

Children practice various conventions of standard English. Children write routinely for a range of tasks, purposes, and audiences.

Name _____

DIRECTIONS Write a word from the box to match each picture.

| towel | snow | couch | soup |

1.

2.

3.

4.

Write the word to finish each sentence. Remember to use a capital letter at the beginning of a sentence.

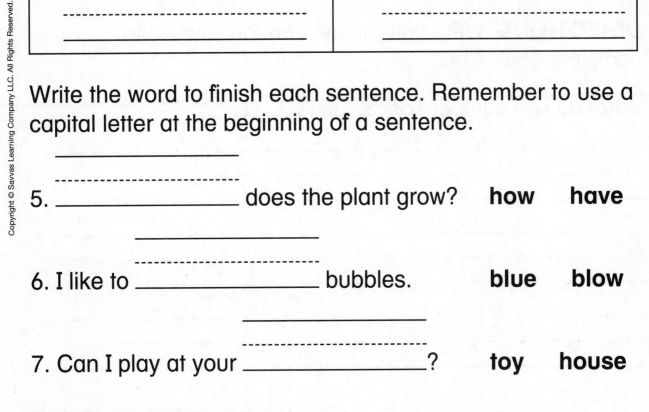

5. _____ does the plant grow? **how** **have**

6. I like to _____ bubbles. **blue** **blow**

7. Can I play at your _____? **toy** **house**

 Children apply grade-level phonics and word analysis skills.

Name _____

DIRECTIONS Choose a word from below and draw it in the box. Then write a sentence using the word.

picnic   overcoat

Write in Response to Reading

DIRECTIONS Write your answer on the lines. Use complete sentences.

What do you think of Tony's family?

Children demonstrate contextual understanding of Benchmark Vocabulary. Children read text closely and use text evidence in their written answers.

Name _____

DIRECTIONS Write the dates correctly.

_____

july 4 1776 _____

_____

may 5 2005 _____

Writing

DIRECTIONS Circle the correct word. Then complete the sentence about *A Picnic in October*. Write information from the book that supports your opinion.

_____

I liked / disliked _____

_____

_____

_____

_____

_____

_____

_____

_____

_____

_____

Children practice various conventions of standard English. Children write routinely for a range of tasks, purposes, and audiences.

Name _____

DIRECTIONS Choose a word from below and draw it in the box. Then write a sentence using the word.

cousins   ferry   island

_____

Write in Response to Reading

DIRECTIONS Write your answer on the lines.

On page 10, the family gets in line. What are they waiting for?

_____

_____

_____

Children demonstrate contextual understanding of Benchmark Vocabulary. Children read text closely and use text evidence in their written answers.

Name _____

DIRECTIONS Read the sentences from *A Picnic in October*.
Circle the words that describe something.

She's wearing her bright green coat.

The wind ruffles the fake fur collar around her neck.

Across on the island, the Statue of Liberty stands, white
and gleaming.

Mike's holding the cake now, in its see-through container.

Write a sentence to describe the people waiting in line on
pages 10 and 11.

_____

_____

_____

_____

_____

_____

_____

Children analyze and respond to literary texts.

Name _____

DIRECTIONS Circle the word that tells who the family belongs to.

Tony's family went on a picnic in October.

DIRECTIONS Write an introduction to your book review. Name the book. Tell about the book. Write your opinion.

_____

- - - - - - - - - - - - - - - - - - - -

_____

- - - - - - - - - - - - - - - - - - - -

_____

- - - - - - - - - - - - - - - - - - - -

_____

- - - - - - - - - - - - - - - - - - - -

_____

- - - - - - - - - - - - - - - - - - - -

_____

- - - - - - - - - - - - - - - - - - - -

_____

- - - - - - - - - - - - - - - - - - - -

_____

Children practice various conventions of standard English. Children write routinely for a range of tasks, purposes, and audiences.

Name _____

DIRECTIONS Circle the word for each picture.

1.	2.	3.
lesson lemon	bacon basket	came camel
4.	5.	6.
cabin cab	timber tiger	river rigged

Draw a picture for each word.

7. spider

8. baby

 Children apply grade-level phonics and word analysis skills.

Name _____

DIRECTIONS Choose a word from below and draw it in the box. Then write a sentence using the word.

understand   disapproving

Write in Response to Reading

DIRECTIONS Read page 13 in *A Picnic in October*. Why does the woman feel better at the end of the page?

Children demonstrate contextual understanding of Benchmark Vocabulary. Children read text closely and use text evidence in their written answers.

Name _____

DIRECTIONS Look at pages 12 through 14 of *A Picnic in October*. Write one detail about a character on these pages.

_____

_____

_____

_____

_____

Write one detail about the events on these pages.

_____

_____

_____

_____

_____

Children analyze and respond to literary text.

Name _____

DIRECTIONS Write the two sentences as one sentence.
Then add a detail.

We went on a picnic. It was fun.

_____

- -

_____

- -

_____

- -

_____

Writing

DIRECTIONS Write at least one reason to support your
opinion for your book report.

_____

- -

_____

- -

_____

- -

_____

- -

Children practice various conventions of standard
English. Children write routinely for a range of tasks,
purposes, and audiences.

Name _____

DIRECTIONS Choose a word from below and draw it in the box. Then write a sentence using the word.

entered   offended

_____

- -

_____

Write in Response to Reading

DIRECTIONS Complete the sentence.

_____

- - - - - - - - - - - - - - - - -

I would like to go to Liberty Island because _____

_____

- -

_____

- -

_____

- -

_____

- -

_____

Children demonstrate contextual understanding of Benchmark Vocabulary. Children read text closely and use text evidence in their written answers.

Name _____

DIRECTIONS Circle the word in ( ) to complete the sentence.

(This / Those) park is a good place for a picnic.

DIRECTIONS Write an ending to your writing from Lessons 7 and 8. Be sure to restate your opinion.

_____

_____

_____

_____

_____

_____

_____

_____

Children practice various conventions of standard English. Children write routinely for a range of tasks, purposes, and audiences.

Name _____

DIRECTIONS Choose a word from below and draw it in the box. Then write a sentence using the word.

gazes   barrier

Write in Response to Reading

DIRECTIONS Complete the sentence.

I think Lady Liberty is _____

Children demonstrate contextual understanding of Benchmark Vocabulary. Children read text closely and use text evidence in their written answers.

Name _____

DIRECTIONS Write the two sentences as one sentence. Then add a detail.

A band played. We listened to music.

_____

- -

_____

- -

_____

- -

_____

Writing

DIRECTIONS Add more details or combine sentences in your writing. Write the new sentence below.

_____

- -

_____

- -

_____

- -

_____

Children practice various conventions of standard English. Children write routinely for a range of tasks, purposes, and audiences.

Name _____

DIRECTIONS Circle the word for each picture.

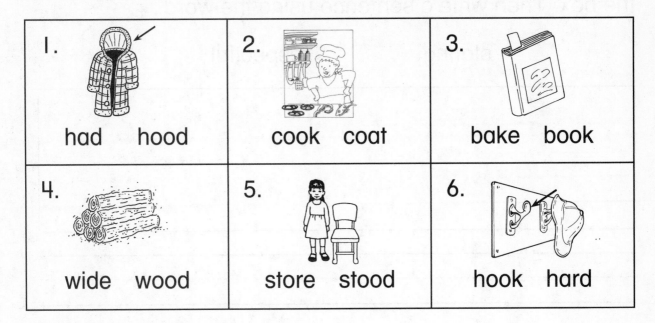

1. had   hood

2. cook   coat

3. bake   book

4. wide   wood

5. store   stood

6. hook   hard

Read the words in the box.
Circle the words that have the same vowel sound as .
Pick one of these words to finish each sentence.

take	foot	took	soon	goat	tool	good

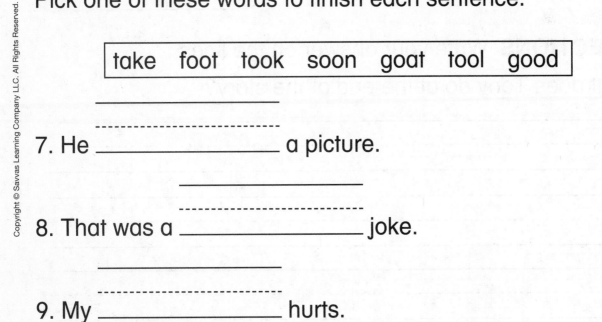

7. He _____ a picture.

8. That was a _____ joke.

9. My _____ hurts.

Children apply grade-level phonics and
word analysis skills.

Name _____

DIRECTIONS Choose a word from below and draw it in the box. Then write a sentence using the word.

staring   respectful

_____

- -

_____

Write in Response to Reading

DIRECTIONS Write your answer on the lines.

What does Tony do at the end of the story?

_____

- -

_____

- -

_____

- -

_____

- -

_____

 Children demonstrate contextual understanding of Benchmark Vocabulary. Children read text closely and use text evidence in their written answers.

Name _____

What is the central message of *A Picnic in October*?

_____

_____

_____

_____

Retell three details that show that message.

_____

----

1. _____

_____

_____

_____

2. _____

_____

_____

_____

----

3. _____

_____

_____

_____

Children analyze and respond to literary text.

Name _____

DIRECTIONS Find the mistake. Write the sentence correctly.

Grandpas hat is black.

_____

- -

_____

Writing

DIRECTIONS Add a detail to your book report using a peer's suggestion.

_____

- -

_____

- -

_____

- -

_____

- -

_____

- -

_____

- -

Children practice various conventions of standard English. Children write routinely for a range of tasks, purposes, and audiences.

Name _____

DIRECTIONS Choose a word from below and draw it in the box. Then write a sentence using the word.

traditional　　celebrates　　island

```
┌─────────────────────────────────────────────┐
│                                             │
│                                             │
│                                             │
│                                             │
│                                             │
└─────────────────────────────────────────────┘
```

_____

_____

Write in Response to Reading

DIRECTIONS Write your answer on the lines.

What traditions can Ama, Raul, and Tony teach each other?

_____

_____

_____

_____

_____

Children demonstrate contextual understanding of Benchmark Vocabulary. Children read text closely and use text evidence in their written answers.

Name _____

DIRECTIONS Find the mistakes.
Write the sentence correctly.

We stand in lin to tak the ferry.

_____
- -
_____
_____
- -
_____

Writing

DIRECTIONS Read your book review. Look for any mistakes in spelling, capital letters, or end punctuation.

Put a check mark in each box to show you have checked for mistakes in your review.

❑ I checked the spelling of every word.

❑ I checked that the author's name is spelled correctly.

❑ I wrote the title of the book correctly.

❑ I used a capital letter at the beginning of each sentence.

❑ I used a capital letter at the beginning of each name.

❑ I capitalized the word *I* every time I used it.

❑ I put an end mark at the end of each sentence.

Children practice various conventions of standard English. Children write routinely for a range of tasks, purposes, and audiences.

Name _____

DIRECTIONS Add **-s, -ed,** or **-ing** to the word in ( ).
Write the new word on the line.

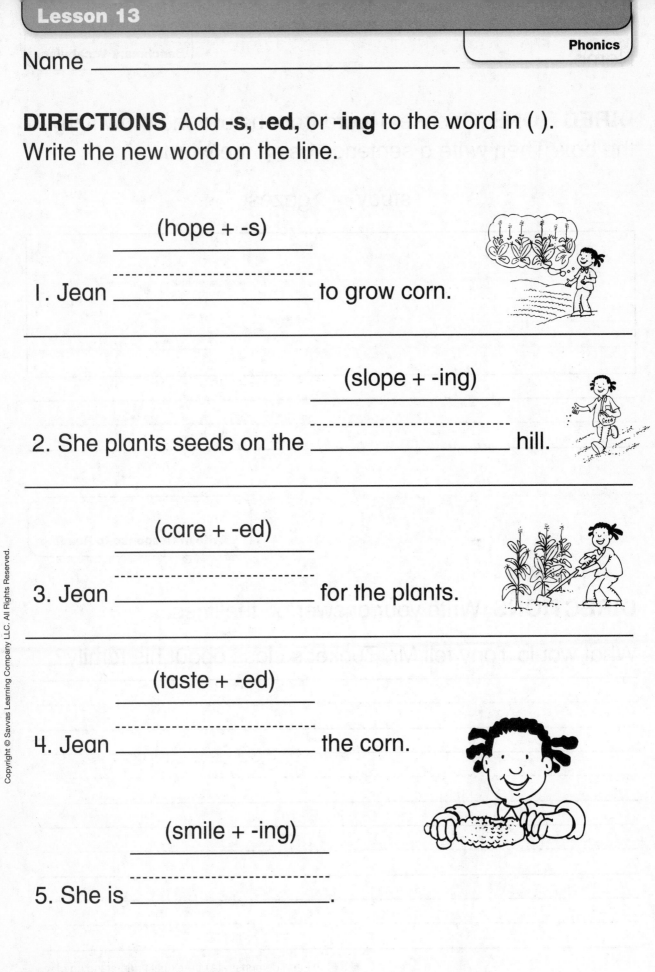

(hope + -s)

_____

1. Jean _____ to grow corn.

(slope + -ing)

_____

2. She plants seeds on the _____ hill.

(care + -ed)

_____

3. Jean _____ for the plants.

(taste + -ed)

_____

4. Jean _____ the corn.

(smile + -ing)

_____

5. She is _____.

Children apply grade-level phonics and word
analysis skills.

Name _____

DIRECTIONS Choose a word from below and draw it in the box. Then write a sentence using the word.

study   gazes

_____

- -

_____

Write in Response to Reading

DIRECTIONS Write your answer on the lines.

What would Tony tell Mr. Tucker's class about his family?

_____

- -

_____

- -

_____

- -

_____

- -

_____

Children demonstrate contextual understanding of Benchmark Vocabulary. Children read text closely and use text evidence in their written answers.

Lesson 13

Name _____

Sleuth Passage

Welcome to Pilsen

Pilsen is part of Chicago. It has a rich history. People from many parts of the world live in Pilsen. In the 1950s, many people from Mexico began to move here. They came to find work. They came to help their families. They brought their favorite music and foods. They brought their traditions. They also brought their love of art!

The Mexican American community has created beautiful murals. A mural is a large painting on a wall. You can see these murals on schools and churches. They are on bridges and in parks. You can even see them on apartment buildings and houses. Pilsen is a work of art!

Many of the murals show important ideas. They show Mexican history and heroes. You see pictures of people working hard. One mural shows a family cooking a meal. Mexican culture is alive and well in Pilsen!

Children read text closely to determine what the text says.

Look for Clues
Underline three details that tell what the murals show.

Ask Questions
Write one question you would like to ask an artist in Pilsen.

_____

_____

_____

Make Your Case
Circle feeling words that help you understand how the
author feels about Pilsen. Then write how the author feels.

_____

_____

_____

Make Your Case: Extend Your Ideas
Why is Pilsen a special place? Use details from the
passage.

_____

_____

_____

_____

 Children read text closely to determine what the text
says.

Name _____

DIRECTIONS Fill in the missing word.

_____

Looking at _____ Statue of Liberty
makes me proud.

DIRECTIONS Write a title for your book review.

_____
_____
_____
_____
_____
_____
_____
_____

 Children practice various conventions of
standard English. Children write routinely for a
range of tasks, purposes, and audiences.

Phonics

DIRECTIONS Circle the word for each picture.

1. coins canes	2. bay boy	3. boil bail
4. joy jay	5. foil fail	6. round royal

Pick a word to finish each sentence.
Write the word on the line.

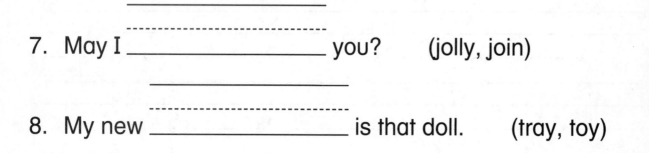

7. May I _____ you?   (jolly, join)

8. My new _____ is that doll.   (tray, toy)

Children apply grade-level phonics and word analysis skills.

Name _____

DIRECTIONS Choose a word from below and draw it in the box. Then write a sentence using the word.

fair   booths   explore

```
┌────────────────────────────────────────────┐
│                                            │
│                                            │
│                                            │
│                                            │
│                                            │
│                                            │
└────────────────────────────────────────────┘
```

_____

- -

_____

Write in Response to Reading

DIRECTIONS Draw a picture of one of the stands at the fair. Write a sentence to tell about the stand.

```
┌────────────────────────────────────────────┐
│                                            │
│                                            │
│                                            │
│                                            │
│                                            │
└────────────────────────────────────────────┘
```

_____

- -

_____

- -

_____

Children demonstrate contextual understanding of Benchmark Vocabulary. Children read text closely and use text evidence in their written answers.

Name _____

DIRECTIONS Circle the correct word.

Look at all (this / these) people!

Where should we put (this / these) box?

Writing

DIRECTIONS Name the topic. Then write your opinion about the topic.

_____

- -

_____

- -

_____

- -

_____

- -

_____

- -

_____

 Children practice various conventions of standard English. Children write routinely for a range of tasks, purposes, and audiences.

Name _____

DIRECTIONS Choose a word from below and draw it in the box. Then write a sentence using the word.

delicious   peered   mischief

DIRECTIONS Write your answer on the lines.

What is a culture fair?

Children demonstrate contextual understanding of Benchmark Vocabulary. Children read text closely and use text evidence in their written answers.

Unit 6 • Module B • Lesson 2 • 417

Lesson 2

Name _____

DIRECTIONS Circle the correct word.

That was (the / a) best movie I ever saw!

I just read (the / a) book about plants.

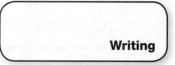

Writing

DIRECTIONS Think about your opinion from Lesson 1.
Write to tell why you feel this way.

_____

- -

_____

- -

_____

_____

- -

_____

_____

- -

_____

_____

- -

_____

Children practice various conventions of standard
English. Children write routinely for a range of tasks,
purposes, and audiences.

Name _____

DIRECTIONS Write a word from the box to match each picture.

| baker | sailor | painter | teacher |

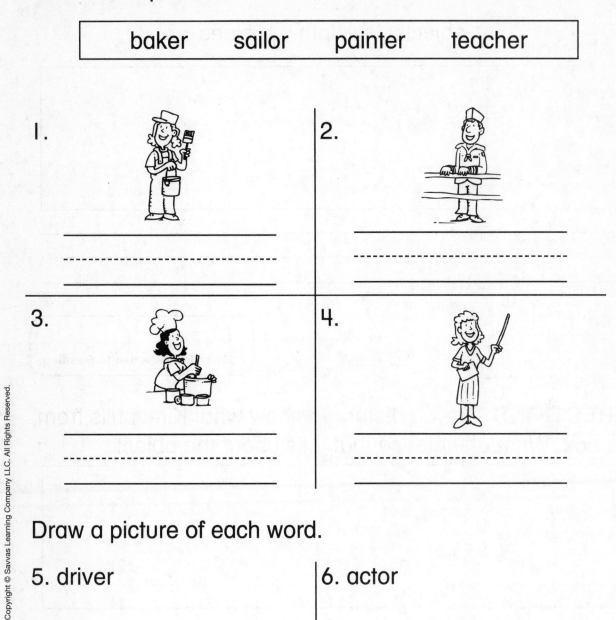

1.

_____
- -
_____

2.

_____
- -
_____

3.

_____
- -
_____

4.

_____
- -
_____

Draw a picture of each word.

5. driver

6. actor

 Children apply grade-level phonics and word analysis skills.

Name _____

DIRECTIONS Choose a word from below and draw it in the box. Then write a sentence using the word.

objects   cloth   clues

_____

- -

_____

Write in Response to Reading

DIRECTIONS Draw a picture to show what Kimi pulls from the box. Write a sentence that tells about the object.

_____

- -

_____

- -

_____

Children demonstrate contextual understanding of Benchmark Vocabulary. Children read text closely and use text evidence in their written answers.

Name _____

DIRECTIONS Choose a word from the story. Write the word. Then write your responses on the lines.

_____

Word: _____

What is the meaning of the word?

_____

_____

_____

Write a sentence that uses the word to tell about something in real life.

_____

_____

_____

_____

_____

 Children analyze and respond to literary texts.

Name _____

DIRECTIONS Write these two sentences as one sentence.

It's summer! I'm so happy!

_____
- -
_____
_____
- -
_____

DIRECTIONS Write about activities at the culture fair.
Circle the activity you would enjoy the most.

_____
- -
_____
- -
_____
_____
- -
_____
- -
_____

Children practice various conventions of standard
English. Children write routinely for a range of tasks,
purposes, and audiences.

Name _____

DIRECTIONS Choose a word from below and draw it in the box. Then write a sentence using the word.

puzzled   competition

```




```
_____
- -
_____

Write in Response to Reading

DIRECTIONS Draw a picture of something a person from India might wear. Write a sentence to tell about your picture.

```




```
_____
- -
_____
- -
_____

Children demonstrate contextual understanding of Benchmark Vocabulary. Children read text closely and use text evidence in their written answers.

Name _____

DIRECTIONS Write today's date.

_____

_____

_____

DIRECTIONS Look for details that support your opinion. Write the details and where you found them.

_____

_____

_____

_____

_____

_____

_____

Children practice various conventions of standard English. Children write routinely for a range of tasks, purposes, and audiences.

Name _____

DIRECTIONS Choose a word from below and draw it in the box. Then write a sentence using the word.

behind   spotted   meetings

DIRECTIONS Draw a picture of the object Maria pulls from the box. Then write a sentence about the object.

Children demonstrate contextual understanding of Benchmark Vocabulary. Children read text closely and use text evidence in their written answers.

DIRECTIONS Think about what happens in this part of the story. Draw the events in order.

Children analyze and respond to literary texts.

Name _____

DIRECTIONS Write the correct word: **and or but.**

_____

Do you want a dog, _____ do you want a cat?

DIRECTIONS Begin writing your opinion piece.

_____

_____

_____

_____

_____

_____

_____

_____

Children practice various conventions of standard English. Children write routinely for a range of tasks, purposes, and audiences.

Name _____

DIRECTIONS Circle the word for each picture.

1. pail paw	2. yawn yard	3. stray straw
4. face faucet	5. auto ace	6. lane lawn

Pick a word to finish each sentence. Circle the word. Write the word in the sentence.

7. I like to eat red _____.

                sauce   sash

8. The bear uses its _____ to catch fish.

                clay   claw

 Children apply grade-level phonics and word analysis skills.

Name _____

DIRECTIONS Choose a word from below and draw it in the box. Then write a sentence using the word.

shiny   polished   hollows

Write in Response to Reading

DIRECTIONS Complete the sentence.

One thing Maria and Kimi pull out of the box is

Children demonstrate contextual understanding of Benchmark Vocabulary. Children read text closely and use text evidence in their written answers.

Unit 6 • Module B • Lesson 6 • 429

Name _____

DIRECTIONS Write the correct word: **so** **because.**

_____

I was tired, _____ I took a nap.

DIRECTIONS Write at least one reason for your opinion.

_____
- -
_____
- -
_____
- -
_____
- -
_____
- -
_____
- -
_____

 Children practice various conventions of standard English. Children write routinely for a range of tasks, purposes, and audiences.

Name _____

DIRECTIONS Choose a word from below and draw it in the box. Then write a sentence using the word.

peeped   handle   detectives

Write in Response to Reading

DIRECTIONS Draw a picture that shows how the story ends. Then write a sentence to tell about the ending.

Children demonstrate contextual understanding of Benchmark Vocabulary. Children read text closely and use text evidence in their written answers.

Name _____

DIRECTIONS Circle the words that tell where something is.

The paper is on the desk.

The trees in the park are so big!

DIRECTIONS Write an ending for your opinion piece.

_____
- -
_____
- -
_____
- -
_____
- -
_____
- -
_____
- -
_____

Children practice various conventions of standard English. Children write routinely for a range of tasks, purposes, and audiences.

Name _____

DIRECTIONS Circle the word that names each picture.

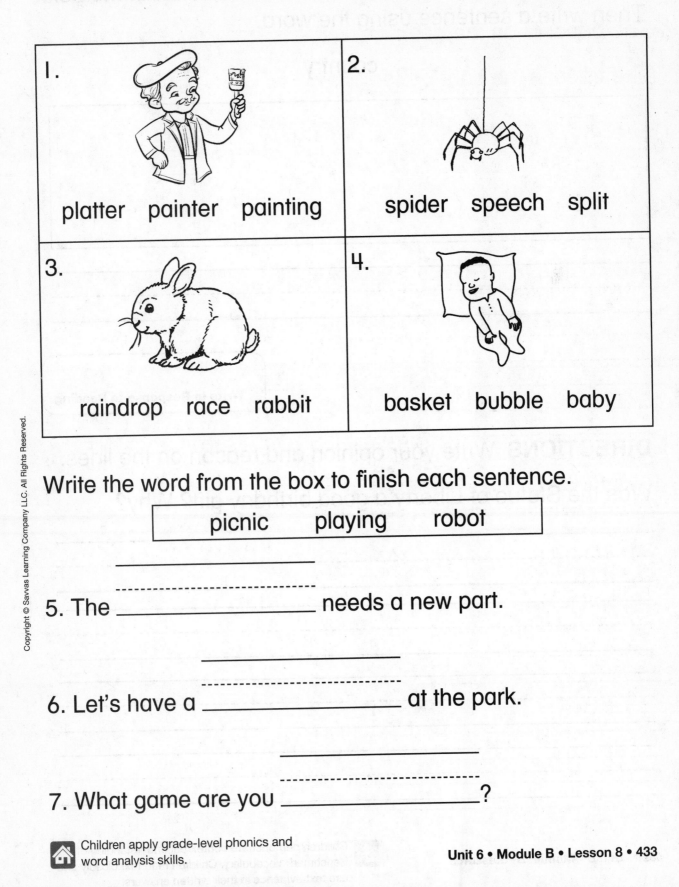

1. platter   painter   painting

2. spider   speech   split

3. raindrop   race   rabbit

4. basket   bubble   baby

Write the word from the box to finish each sentence.

| picnic   playing   robot |

5. The _____ needs a new part.

6. Let's have a _____ at the park.

7. What game are you _____?

Children apply grade-level phonics and word analysis skills.

Name _____

DIRECTIONS Draw a picture of the word below in the box. Then write a sentence using the word.

country

Write in Response to Reading

DIRECTIONS Write your opinion and reason on the lines.

Was the Statue of Liberty a good birthday gift? Why?

Children demonstrate contextual understanding of Benchmark Vocabulary. Children read text closely and use text evidence in their written answers.

Name _____

The Festival

My school had a world festival. I think every school should have one. We celebrated different countries and cultures around the world. The best part was the music. I liked dancing to the music, too. I even played music!

My friend Jose is from Puerto Rico. He shared neat things about his homeland. People speak Spanish there. They eat fruits like guava and mango. They dance to salsa music. Jose let me try the maracas. I like the sound they make when they shake.

I learned about other places around the world at the festival. I heard different languages. I saw instruments that made different sounds. I ate food that was new to me.

I know that people are different. People come from different places around the world. We all live in America. Being different makes our country strong. It makes it special.

Children read text closely to determine what the text says.

Look for Clues

Underline the sentence that tells why the writer thinks every school should have a world festival.

Look for Clues: Extend Your Ideas

In the writer's opinion, what was the best part of the festival? Circle the sentence. Draw a box around the writer's reasons for this opinion.

Ask Questions

What questions would you ask the writer about the world festival?

_____

- -

_____

- -

_____

Ask Questions: Extend Your Ideas

Suppose you wonder what the writer learned about Puerto Rico. Underline the sentences that answer that question.

Make Your Case

What event at this world festival would you enjoy? Underline the event or activity in the third paragraph. Then write reasons from the text to tell why.

_____

- -

_____

- -

_____

 Children read text closely to determine what the text says.

Name _____

DIRECTIONS Finish the sentence.

I like to play games and _____

_____

DIRECTIONS Think about details you can add to your writing. Rewrite your opinion piece.

_____

_____

_____

_____

_____

_____

_____

_____

_____

Children practice various conventions of standard English. Children write routinely for a range of tasks, purposes, and audiences.

Name _____

DIRECTIONS Draw a picture of the word below in the box. Then write a sentence using the word.

believe

Write in Response to Reading

DIRECTIONS Write your answer on the lines.

What does the Statue of Liberty stand for?

Children demonstrate contextual understanding of Benchmark Vocabulary. Children read text closely and use text evidence in their written answers.

Name _____

DIRECTIONS Add an end mark to each sentence.

What is our country's birthday

It is the Fourth of July

Writing

DIRECTIONS Write to tell how you will publish your opinion piece.

_____
- -
_____
- -
_____
- -
_____
- -
_____
- -
_____
- -
_____

Children practice various conventions of standard English. Children write routinely for a range of tasks, purposes, and audiences.

Name _____

DIRECTIONS Choose a word from below and draw it in the box. Then write a sentence using the word.

puzzle   hope

DIRECTIONS Write your opinion and reason on the lines.

Which do you think is a better symbol for America: the American flag or the Statue of Liberty? Why?

Children demonstrate contextual understanding of Benchmark Vocabulary. Children read text closely and use text evidence in their written answers.

Name _____

DIRECTIONS Circle the words that need an uppercase letter.

new york city has parades every year on july 4.

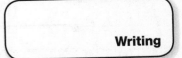

Writing

DIRECTIONS Name the topic. Then write your opinion about the topic.

_____
- -
_____
- -
_____
- -
_____
- -
_____
- -
_____

 Children practice various conventions of standard English. Children write routinely for a range of tasks, purposes, and audiences.

Lesson 11

Name _____

DIRECTIONS Add **re-** or **un-** to the word in ( ).
Write the new word on the line.

(build)
_____

1. Mr. Ford will _____ the car.

_____

(happy)
_____

2. He is _____ with the color.

(paint)
_____

3. He will _____ it.

_____

(fills)
_____

4. He _____ the car with gas.

_____

(lock)
_____

5. Don't forget to _____ the door!

 Children apply grade-level phonics and word
analysis skills.

Name _____

DIRECTIONS Choose a word from below and draw it in the box. Then write a sentence using the word.

cloth   competition   believe

[box for drawing]

_____

_____

Write in Response to Reading

DIRECTIONS Think about what you learned in *Whose Is This?* and *L Is for Liberty*. Write your answer on the lines.

What can you tell about the people who live in America?

_____

_____

_____

_____

Children demonstrate contextual understanding of Benchmark Vocabulary. Children read text closely and use text evidence in their written answers.

DIRECTIONS Write to tell how *Whose Is This?* and *L Is for Liberty* are different.

_____

- -

_____

- -

_____

- -

_____

- -

_____

- -

_____

- -

_____

- -

_____

- -

_____

- -

_____

- -

_____

Children analyze and respond to literary and informational texts.

Lesson 11

Name _____

Conventions

DIRECTIONS Write the sentence again. Use pronouns for the underlined words.

<u>The immigrants</u> thought <u>the Statue of Liberty</u> was a welcome sight.

_____

- -

_____

- -

_____

Writing

DIRECTIONS Write reasons for your opinion.

_____

- -

_____

- -

_____

- -

_____

- -

_____

Children practice various conventions of standard English. Children write routinely for a range of tasks, purposes, and audiences.

Name _____

DIRECTIONS Choose a word from below and draw it in the box. Then write a sentence using the word.

peered   hope

_____

_____

Write in Response to Reading

DIRECTIONS Think about what you learned in *Whose Is This?* and *L Is for Liberty*. Write your answer on the lines.

What is one thing you learned about immigrants?

_____

_____

_____

Children demonstrate contextual understanding of Benchmark Vocabulary. Children read text closely and use text evidence in their written answers.

Name _____

Choose a word or phrase from *Whose Is This?* Write it on the line.

What is the meaning of the word or phrase?

Write a sentence that uses the word or phrase.

Choose a word or phrase from *L Is for Liberty*. Write it on the line.

What is the meaning of the word or phrase?

Write a sentence that uses the word or phrase.

Children analyze and respond to literary and informational texts.

Name _____

DIRECTIONS Add **un** or **re**. Then write the meaning of the word.

_____
_____ **tie**

_____
_____
_____

Add **ful** or **less**. Then write the meaning of the word.

_____
color _____

_____
_____

DIRECTIONS Write an ending for your opinion piece.

_____
_____
_____
_____
_____

Children practice various conventions of standard English. Children write routinely for a range of tasks, purposes, and audiences.

DIRECTIONS Circle the word for each picture.

1. gold good	2. child chilled	3. past post
4. fin find	5. wind went	6. old all

Circle the word to finish each sentence.

7. I told / tied my baby sister a story.

8. I can't fine / find my pencil.

Children apply grade-level phonics and word
analysis skills.